"An awesomely learned and, at times, touchingly personal discussion of the ancient origins of such New Age marvels as angels, prophetic dreams and near-death experiences which figure prominently in accounts of the end of time."

—*Newsday*

"If there is a critical mind alive today and writing in the English language more important than Harold Bloom's, I have not heard the case made effectively . . . [*Omens of Millennium*] is so beautifully written, so sparely argued, so marvelously full of the revelation of an acute mind at work, that it is not hard to read . . . Here is an exquisite intellect working with exquisite discipline to produce exquisite clarity."

—*The Baltimore Sun*

"Some time back Harold Bloom remarked, with ill-concealed relish, that novelist William Styron had once dismissed him as just a 'school teacher.' This is like referring to a nuclear-powered aircraft carrier as just a boat: Yes, Harold Bloom has been a professor of English at Yale for the past forty years, but he is also . . . the best-known and most controversial American literary critic of his generation . . . Bloom is a visionary critic, a reader who peers deeply into the soul of poems and writers and himself. *Omens of Millennium* is . . . a provocative book, shot through with wide learning, hard thinking and disturbing ideas . . . Harold Bloom takes seriously our millennial obsessions and searchingly explores our spiritual natures, while reminding us that we Americans are, as Emerson remarked with his usual insight, 'all poets and mystics.'"

—Michael Dirda,
Civilization

"This is an engaging and refreshing book. It is also a necessary one, in that it may help to reintroduce the texture of the spiritual world within the increasingly tattered fabric of material reality. That is why Professor Bloom's perceptions are so important and, in a millenarian setting, so timely."

—Peter Ackroyd,
The London Times

continued . . .

"The questions [Bloom] raises are fascinating, and readers who join him on his voyage of exploration will find the journey difficult, but rewarding."

—*Literary Review*

"*Omens of Millennium* is born of despair, but focuses throughout on possibility, with a true teacher's refusal to give up the job of stimulating and informing, no matter how restless the class."

—Marina Warner,
The Washington Post Book World

"*Omens of Millennium* is [Bloom's] spiritual autobiography, a fascinating exploration in comparative religion and literature which, among other things, helps us to appreciate the origins and various understandings of these unique phenomena through the centuries . . . Bloom's learned but remarkably readable discussion of these matters is masterly . . . His book is so rich in stimulating thought and in acquainting us with approaches and connections between those who lived centuries ago and our world."

—*Bookpage*

"A dazzling, maverick study . . . a tour de force, highlighting a secret history of mystical thought whose visionaries and poets call out to each other over the centuries."

—*Publishers Weekly*
(starred review)

"Entertaining and provocative."

—*The Philadelphia Inquirer*

"Full of dazzling insights and unexpected connections."

—*The Economist*

"A personal spiritual testament as well as an exploration of the Gnostics of the distant past . . . a wonderful journey."

—*The Hartford Courant*

"Harold Bloom's latest work of religious and literary criticism places America's recent obsession with spiritual phenomena, angels, near-death experiences, and dream interpretation in the historical context of Judaism, Christianity, and Islam. Bloom succeeds in writing a comprehensive, concise, and witty commentary on these topics. Bloom, the sixty-five-year-old author of twenty-one previous works of criticism, uses his highly refined understanding of the Bible, the Kabbalah, the Dead Sea Scrolls, the Koran, and other religious texts to demonstrate how the world's great religions drew from the gnostic and Zoroastrian spirituality the spiritual themes that are being crudely revived in the popular culture of the U.S. today . . . His humor and cogency preserve this terrific thesis for general interest."

—*Booklist*

"Informed and lively . . . Having sketched a consistently interesting history of the various forms of ancient gnosis, Bloom offers his version as an alternative. It's a daring gesture, especially if we keep in mind that he's not after a New Age audience, but is appealing to readers serious about belief in an ironic and skeptical era."

—*Toronto Globe and Mail*

"*Omens* is informed by the same remarkable mastery of arts and letters that Bloom displayed with such assurance in *The Western Canon* . . . [B]y the end of *Omens*, it is clear that intellectual freedom rather than spiritual enlightenment is what Bloom values and seeks. And we realize, too, that a man as refined and yet unfettered as Bloom could not have found his way to any expression of spirituality that is less elegant, less exalted or less demanding of true belief than the one he has chosen."

—*Los Angeles Times Book Review*

OMENS OF MILLENNIUM

The Gnosis of Angels, Dreams, and Resurrection

HAROLD BLOOM

RIVERHEAD BOOKS
New York

RIVERHEAD BOOKS
Published by The Berkley Publishing Group
200 Madison Avenue
New York, New York 10016

Excerpts from *The Gospel of Truth*. Translation copyright © 1980 by Bentley Layton. Reprinted by permission of the translator.

Copyright © 1996 by Harold Bloom
Book design by Marysarah Quinn
Cover design by David Eldridge/Senate Design Limited
Cover art: Alessandro Allori, *Allegory of Life*, oil on copper. Galleria degli Uffizi, Florence/The Bridgeman Art Library, London

Riverhead hardcover edition: September 1996
First Riverhead trade paperback edition: October 1997
Riverhead trade paperback ISBN: 1-57322-629-7

The Putnam Berkley World Wide Web site address is http://www.berkley.com

The Library of Congress has catalogued the Riverhead hardcover edition as follows:

Bloom, Harold.
    Omens of Millennium : the gnosis of angels,
dreams, and resurrection / Harold Bloom.
        p.   cm.
    ISBN 1-57322-045-0 (alk. paper)
    1. Bloom, Harold.   2. Gnosticism.   3. Angels—
Comparative studies.   4. Dreams—Religious
aspects—Comparative studies.   5. Future life—
Comparative studies.   6. Resurrection–Comparative
studies.   7. Millennialism—Comparative studies.
8. United States—Religion.
I. Title.
BF1999.B65146   1996   96-3868   CIP
291.2'3—dc20

PRINTED IN THE UNITED STATES OF AMERICA
10 9 8 7 6 5 4 3 2 1

FOR
GLEN HARTLEY
AND
LYNN CHU

Contents

Man is in a trap . . . and goodness avails him nothing in the new dispensation. There is nobody now to care one way or the other. Good and evil, pessimism and optimism—are a question of blood group, not angelic disposition. Whoever it was that used to heed us and care for us, who had concern for our fate and the world's, has been replaced by another who glories in our servitude to matter, and to the basest part of our own natures.

—Lawrence Durrell,
Monsieur, or The Prince of Darkness

OMENS OF MILLENNIUM

INTRODUCTION

The dominant element in Western religious traditions—particularly in Europe and the Middle East, less so in America—tends to be institutional, historical, and dogmatic in its orientations. This is true for normative Judaism, for Islam in its Sunni and Shi'ite branches, and for Christianity, whether Roman Catholic, Eastern Orthodox, or mainline Protestant. In all of these, God essentially is regarded as external to the self. There are mystics and spiritual visionaries within these traditions who have been able to reconcile themselves with institutional authority, but there always has been an alternative convention, the way of Gnosis, an acquaintance with, or knowledge of, the God within, that has been condemned as heretical

1

by the institutional faiths. In one form or another, Gnosis has maintained itself for at least the two millennia of what we have learned to call the Common Era, shared first by Jews and Christians, and then by Muslims also. My own religious experience and conviction is a form of Gnosis, and in some sense all of this book, and not just its coda, is a kind of Gnostic sermon. My spiritual concerns, while personal, Jewish, and American, have a universal element in them that stems from a lifetime's study of Gnosis, both ancient and modern. Yet this book, though informed by scholarship, is not a scholarly work but a personal religious testimony that reaches out to our common concerns as Millennium approaches.

I seek to show how four of our increasing concerns are necessarily fused: angelology, a quasi-predictive element in dreams, the "near-death experience," and the approach of the Millennium (variously placed at the years 2000 or 2001 or 2033). The fusion of these matters long precedes our own moment, and can be traced back to ancient Persia and Palestine, and to medieval Arabia, Provence, and Spain. I have turned to Christian Gnosticism, Muslim Shi'ite Sufism, and Jewish Kabbalism as my explanatory sources because all of them provide cogent interpretations of the links between angels, dreams, otherworldly journeys or astral-body manifestations, and messianic expectations. Other esoteric traditions also comprehend these entities, but perhaps not as vividly nor as relevantly as do the Gnostics, Sufis, and Kabbalists. There seems to be a common, perhaps Hermetist, strand in Gnosis, Sufi theosophy, and Kabbalah, which I have tried to develop here into a mode that might elucidate aspects of the uncanny that now interest many among us,

skeptics and believers alike, as we move towards the twenty-first century.

I have tended to follow only a few major authorities: Hans Jonas and Ioan Couliano for Christian Gnosticism, Henry Corbin for Iranian Sufism, Gershom Scholem and Moshe Idel for Kabbalah, but most of my interpretations of these traditions are by now essentially my own and are overtly affected by my sense of what I call the American Religion, a syncretic and prevalent faith that seems to me very different from European Christianity. Interest in angelology, prophetic dreams, and near-death manifestations as millennial omens is necessarily worldwide, but has a particular intensity in the United States, where the American Christ tends to be the Jesus of the Resurrection, rather than of the Crucifixion or the Ascension. I do not however intend this book to be in any way a sequel to my *The American Religion* (1992), since I concentrate here exclusively upon the interlocking between angels, dreams, not dying, and expectations of the end of our time. A nation whose quasi-official high priest is the Reverend Billy Graham, author of *Approaching Hoofbeats: The Four Horsemen of the Apocalypse*, is rather clearly more likely than most other countries to have strong intimations of the Millennium. Our Southern Baptists and Mormons, our Adventists, Pentecostals, and other indigenous faiths all have particular end-time prospects in view, and I have seen these as part of this book's subject, but only upon its periphery. At the center is a complex of ideas, images, and inner experiences that have taken on outward, visible, palpable forms for many among us. Some of these doubtless are delusionary; some perhaps are not. Yet all of them have distinguished forerunners in venerable traditions that rightly possess both cultural prestige and explanatory power.

Here at the beginning I wish to stress my own conviction that it is fruitless either to literalize or to dismiss spiritual experience, whether ancient, medieval, or contemporary. This conviction is pragmatic, and I follow William James in acknowledging religious experiences that make a difference as being authentic differences: from one another, and among us. For many of the ancients, the phenomena of angels, of dreams, and of otherworldly journeys or astral-body manifestations essentially were one, because what we now call psychology and cosmology also were one. Much of what we now call science is the merest scientism, which in its later nineteenth-century version malformed aspects of Freud's speculations, particularly upon the nature of dreams. At the outer limit of today's physics, a perpetually fading demarcation, speculations abound that nineteenth-century scientism would have dismissed as mystical. It fascinates me that much of our current uncanniness, as the Millennium nears, repeats at a popular level the convictions and images of refined, esoteric sages who illuminate us more than we seem capable of illuminating them. Henry Corbin, the great scholar of Iranian Islam, particularly of the Shi'ite Sufis, deplored the Western gap between sense perception, with its empirical data, and the intuitions or categories of the intellect. Poetic imagination, in post-Enlightenment Western tradition, works in that void, but most of us see the products of such imagination as being only fictions or myths. Corbin eloquently urged otherwise:

On this account there remains no hope for recovering the reality *sui generis* of a suprasensible world which is neither the
empirical world of the senses nor the abstract world of the
intellect. It has furthermore for a long time now seemed to
us radically impossible to rediscover the actual reality—we
would say the *reality in act*—proper to the "Angelic World,"
a reality prescribed in Being itself, not in any way a myth de-
pendent on socio-political or socio-economic infrastruc-
tures. It is impossible to penetrate, in the way in which one
penetrates into a real world, into the universe of the Zoroastrian angelology . . . we would say as much of the angelo-
phanies of the Bible.

> —*Spiritual Body and Celestial Earth*,
> translated by Nancy Pearson
> (Princeton, 1977), pp. *vii–viii*

From Corbin's point of view, following the sages, literal or
empirical sense itself is a metaphor for a lack of vision, which
seems to me pragmatically true enough. Between the sensory
and the intellectual world, sages always have experienced an intermediate realm, one akin to what we call the imaginings of
poets. If you are a religious believer, whether normative or heterodox, this middle world is experienced as the presence of the
divine in our everyday world. If you are more skeptical, such
presence is primarily aesthetic or perhaps a kind of perspectivism. In this book the sphere between literal and intellectual
realities takes its traditional name of the angelic realm, and is
described and analyzed as such. Angels, in the Judaic, Christian,
and Islamic sense, rarely appear in the Hebrew Bible, and

scarcely play independent roles until the very late Book of Daniel, written about 165 B.C.E., the time of the Maccabean uprising against the Syro-Hellenes. In the earliest biblical narrative, the Yahwist or J strand of the tenth century B.C.E., most of the angels are surrogates for Yahweh himself, and probably were added to the text by the Redactor at the time of the return from Babylon or soon afterwards. There is a wry Talmudic adage that "The angels' names came from Babylon," and I suspect that more than their names came from east of the Jordan.

The angelology of Daniel, and of the Books of Enoch after it, is essentially Zoroastrian rather than Israelite. Norman Cohn, an authority upon millennarian thinking, traces its origin to the Iranian prophet Zoroaster, who cannot as yet be precisely dated, but who may go back to 1500 B.C.E., half a millennium before the Yahwist. Zoroaster began as a priest of the ancient Iranian religion of the Magi, but he reformed it, and Zoroastrianism became the faith of the Persian empire from at least the sixth century B.C.E. through the mid-seventh century C.E., when the Muslims drove it out. Today there are only about a hundred thousand or so Zoroastrians, the Parsis, in India, and a few thousand (at most) in Iraq. A major religion has virtually vanished, except to the extent that Judaism, Christianity, and Islam retain the peculiar stamp of Zoroastrian messianism upon them. Zoroaster's god, Ahura Mazda, Lord of Light and Wisdom, was benign and powerful, but had an evil twin, Angra Mainyu, Lord of Evil and Destruction. The ceaseless war between the twins would end, someday, in the triumph of Ahura Mazda, and the establishment of peace and joy forever. As the first millennial

Ahura Mazda vs Angra Mainyu

prophet, Zoroaster can be said to have invented the resurrection of the dead. Before him, everyone was believed to descend to a sad, dreary condition underground, except for a few favored by the gods. In Zoroaster's vision, his believers went to the skies and his opponents to an underground place of punishment. He thus seems to have added hell to his many inventions, as well as the image of the resurrection of the body, when the final time would come. Transfigured by a divine fire, nature would turn into eternity. Evidently Zoroaster expected that this great change would come in his own lifetime. Since this did not happen, the prophet had the foresight to envision a future benefactor or messianic figure, the Saoshyant, who will prevail against all evil forces, and who will resurrect the dead.

Christ figure

In the long history of Zoroastrianism the original doctrines of the prophet proved less important than the revisionary faith of Zurvanism, which began as a heresy but dominated the state religion of the Iranian empire from the start of the fourth century B.C.E. on. Instead of an imminent apocalypse, Zurvanism proposed a cycle of world ages. Three millennia after Zoroaster, Ormazd (the new name for Ahura Mazda) would at last triumph over Ahriman (the final name for the wicked Angra Mainyu). Zurvan, or time, was seen as the father both of Ormazd and Ahriman, an identification that made it easier for Hellenized Judaism to assimilate Zurvanism, since Yahweh could be equated with Zurvan. Norman Cohn traces the influence of Zurvanism from the books of Daniel and of Enoch through the Qumran (Dead Sea) community on to the Revelation of Saint John the Divine. Henry Corbin does the same for the continuity of

Zurvanism and Iranian Islam, particularly the Shi'ite Sufis. Angelology became the largest Zurvanite gift to the Jews, Christians, and Muslims.

I will trace the development of angelology later in this book, but wish to reflect here upon precisely how the origin of the angels in Iranian millennial religion has affected their characteristics ever since. The Hebrew Bible, including Daniel, the last-written of its twenty books, knows nothing of an evil principle independent of God. Satan in the Book of Job is an authorized accuser, sanctioned by Yahweh, and not a devil or a being who can operate of his own will, or for his own purposes. It is in the Pseudepigrapha, from Enoch on, that Satan truly begins his dazzling career as a rebel against God. Yet even in Daniel, within the canon of the Hebrew Bible, the angels begin to be named, and for the first time they prophesy the future, if only by interpreting Daniel's dreams. Michael and Gabriel, guardian angels of Israel, are the prelude (as will be seen) to the angelic avalanche that comes down upon the people of God in the books of Enoch. The central image of Zoroaster's vision is a cleansing and healing fire, which transforms Enoch into Metatron, greatest of the angels, to whom much of this book will be devoted. Metatron, who is crucial in the Kabbalah, particularly in its greatest book, the *Zohar* of Moses de Leon, is an angel unlike any before him in Judaic tradition. He is scarcely Yahweh's servant, and not at all Yahweh's messenger; he is "the lesser Yahweh," a second power in heaven. His ontological status is both god and angel, recalling the Elohim, or divine beings, of whom Yahweh at first was one.

The author of Enoch probably took his starting point from

Zoroastrian cosmology, where the God of Light and Wisdom is always surrounded by six related powers, the Zoroastrian archangels. Ormazd appears with three masculine archangels on his right, and three feminine archangels on his left, while he himself is both father and mother of Creation. Of the six archangels, the most crucial for this book is Spenta Armaita, uniquely the feminine angel of the earth, and the mother of Daena, who is the astral or resurrection body of each of us, manifesting herself to the soul on the dawn that follows the third night after our death. The image of the astral body, or Garment of Light, is older than Zoroastrianism; it goes back at least to the India of the Vedas, and has earlier analogues in Egypt and in immemorial shamanism throughout the world. Yet its Zoroastrian version seems decisive for the West; it blended with Alexandrian Hermetism and Neoplatonism until it attained its full development first in Iranian Sufism and then in Kabbalah. Those elaborate visions I will adumbrate later; here at the start it suffices to ascribe both our angelology and our characteristic "near-death experience" to their authentic origins in the Iranian imagination, both Mazdean and Muslim. It is ironic that Christianity always has regarded Islam as a heresy, and Zoroastrianism as an exotic remnant, while owing much of its spirituality to both rival traditions.

What most strongly links angels, prophetic dreams, and the hope of not dying to millennial yearnings, whether messianic or fearful? My answer would be an image, which in no way implies that what is held in and by the image may not be a reality, larger than those we too readily know. This image is that of a primordial person, at once male and female, earlier than Adam and

9

Eve, unfallen and quasi-divine, angelic and yet higher than the angels, a nostalgic dream yet also a prophecy of millennial or messianic splendor, blazing in fiery light. That image has many names; the best generic one I know is Anthropos, or Man (again meaning female just as much as male). However heterodox this primordial image of Man may seem to normative Judaism, Christianity, and Islam, it also may be the ultimate basis of all those religions. Approaching the Millennium, we encounter numerous omens that will be variations upon the ancient image that, more than any other, breaks down the orthodox antithesis between God and man. Since Iranian Sufism and the Kabbalism that it influenced combine elements of Hermetic Platonism, Christian Gnosticism, and Zurvanism, its image of the Man of Light is both eclectic and central enough to serve the purposes of this book. The guardian angel, or heavenly twin; the dream that is both messenger and self-interpreter; the astral body that is appropriate for the ascent of resurrection; the advent of the end-time: all four of these omens merge in the image of a restored Primordial Man, an epiphany and a witness.

One concern remains for this introduction: Gnosis, or direct acquaintance of God within the self, is esoteric, whether it be Zoroastrian, Hermetic, Christian Gnostic, Muslim Sufi, Jewish Kabbalist, or some mixed, syncretic version of these faiths. In our contemporary world, as we drift towards the Millennium, our pervasive omens are more popular and secular than they are Judaic, Christian, or Muslim. Those among us who feel the presence of angels, who dream forwards, who undergo the "near-death experience," rarely are erudite in ancient esotericisms, or at best know the traditional images in debased forms, adulterations by the New Age. How are we to understand the continuities, frequently apparent and sometimes real, between Gnosis and the everyday? Do people, in the shadow of the Millennium, confront archetypal images that somehow have an independent existence, or do they reenact (and literalize) sacred patterns now reduced to fashions? Do they copy one another or turn within to copy something that is already themselves, the best and oldest elements in their selves?

I am not a Jungian, and so give no credence to the archetypes of a collective unconscious. But I am both a literary and a religious critic, a devoted student of Gnosis both ancient and modern, and I have enormous respect for recurrent images of human spirituality, no matter how they may be transmitted. Images have their own potency and their own persistence; they testify to human need and desire, but also to a transcendent frontier that marks either a limit to the human, or a limitlessness that may be beyond the human. I return here to what I cited earlier, Henry Corbin's "suprasensible world which is neither the empirical world of the sense nor the abstract world of the intellect." In that intermediate world, images reign, whether of the plays of Shakespeare, the scriptures of religion, our dreams, the presence of angels, or astral-body manifestations. The Millennium may be an event only in that middle world, but who can establish or prophesy the ultimate relations between sense impressions, images, and concepts? The angelic world, whether it be metaphor or reality, is a giant image in which we may see and study ourselves, even as we move towards what may be the end of our time.

PRELUDE:
SELF-RELIANCE OR
MERE GNOSTICISM

1.

I am to invite men drenched in Time to recover themselves
and come out of time, and taste their native immortal air.
—RALPH WALDO EMERSON

If you seek *yourself* outside yourself, then you will encounter disaster, whether erotic or ideological. That
must be why Ralph Waldo Emerson, in his central essay, "Self-
Reliance" (1840), remarked that "Traveling is a fool's paradise." I am sixty-five, and it is past time to write my own
version of "Self-Reliance." Spiritual autobiography in our era,
I thought until now, is best when it is implicit. But the moment
comes when you know pretty much what you are going to
know, and when you realize that more living and reading and
brooding will not greatly alter the self. I am in my fortieth consecutive year of teaching at Yale, and my seventh at NYU, and

for the last decade I have taught Shakespeare almost exclusively. Shakespeare, aside from all his other preternatural strengths, gives me the constant impression that he knows more than anyone else ever has known. Most scholars would call that impression an illusion, but to me it seems the pragmatic truth. Knowing myself, knowing Shakespeare, and knowing God are three separate but closely related quests.

Why bring God into it?

Seeking God outside the self courts the disasters of dogma, institutional corruption, historical malfeasance, and cruelty. For at least two centuries now most Americans have sought the God within rather than the God of European Christianity. But why bring Shakespeare into all this, since to me he seems the archetype of the secular writer?

You know the self primarily by knowing yourself; knowing another human being is immensely difficult, perhaps impossible, though in our youth or even our middle years we deceive ourselves about this. Yet this is why we read and listen to Shakespeare: in order to encounter other selves; no other writer can do that for us. We never encounter Shakespeare himself, as we can encounter Dante or Tolstoy in their work. Whether you can encounter God himself or herself depends upon yourself; we differ greatly from one another in that vital regard. But to return to the self: we can know it primarily through our own solitude, or we can know representatives of it, most vividly in Shakespeare, or we can know God in it, but only when indeed it is our own self. Perhaps the greatest mystics, poets, and lovers have been able to know God in another self, but I am skeptical as to whether that possibility still holds at this late time, with the Millennium rushing upon us.

Even the most spiritual of autobiographies is necessarily a song of the self. At sixty-five, I find myself uncertain just when my self was born. I cannot locate it in my earliest memories of childhood, and yet I recall its presence in certain memories of reading, particularly of the poets William Blake and Hart Crane, when I was about nine or ten. In my instance at least, the self came to its belated birth (or second birth) by reading visionary poetry, a reading that implicitly was an act of knowing something previously unknown within me. Only later could that self-revelation become explicit; Blake and Hart Crane, like some other great poets, have the power to awaken their readers to an implicit answering power, to a previously unfelt sense of possibilities for the self. You can call it a sense of "possible sublimity," of "something evermore about to be," as the poet William Wordsworth named it. Emerson, advocating self-trust, asked: "What is the aboriginal Self, on which a universal reliance may be grounded?" His answer was a primal power, or "deep force," that we discover within ourselves. In the eloquence of certain sermons, Emerson found his deep force; for me it came out of exalted passages in Blake and Crane that haunt me still:

> God appears & God is Light
> To those poor Souls who dwell in Night,
> But does a Human Form Display
> To those who Dwell in Realms of Day.
>
> —WILLIAM BLAKE,
> *"Auguries of Innocence"*

And so it was I entered the broken world
To trace the visionary company of love,
   its voice
An instant in the wind (I know not whither
   hurled)
But not for long to hold each desperate choice.
—HART CRANE,
"The Broken Tower"

These days, in our America, so many go about proclaiming "empowerment," by which actually they mean "resentment," or "catering to resentment." To be empowered by eloquence and vision is what Emerson meant by self-reliance, and is the start of what I mean by "mere Gnosticism," where "mere" takes its original meaning of "pure" or "unmixed." To fall in love with great poetry when you are young is to be awakened to the self's potential, in a way that has little to do, initially, with overt knowing. The self's potential as power involves the self's immortality, not as duration but as the awakening to a knowledge of something in the self that cannot die, because it was never born. It is a curious sensation when a young person realizes that she or he is not altogether the child of that person's natural parents. Freud reduced such a sensation to "the changeling fantasy," in which you imagine you are a faery child, plucked away by adoptive parents who then masquerade as a natural mother and father. But is it only a fantasy to locate, in the self, a magical or occult element, older than any other component of the self? Deep reading in childhood was once the norm for many among us; visual and auditory overstimulation now makes such reading very rare, and I suspect that changeling fantasies are

As a child — I understood this well.

16

vanishing together with the experience of early, authentic reading. At more than half a century away from the deep force of first reading and loving poetry, I no longer remember precisely *what* I then felt, and yet can recall *how* it felt. It was an elevation, a mounting high on no intoxicants except incantatory language, but of a rather different sort than contemporary hip-hop. The language of Blake and Hart Crane, of Marlowe and Shakespeare and Milton, transcended its rush of glory, its high, excited verbal music, and gave the pleasures of excited thought, of a thinking that changed one's outer nature, while opening up an inner identity, a self within the self, previously unknown.

2.

Gilbert Keith Chesterton, shrewdest of modern Catholic writers, warned, "[T]hat Jones shall worship the god within him turns out ultimately to mean that Jones shall worship Jones." Mere Gnosticism badly needs to be distinguished from such large self-worship; Bloom does not wish to worship Bloom, that after all not being much of a religious experience. Our contemporary debasement of Gnosticism goes under the name of the New Age, a panoply wide enough to embrace Shirley MacLaine and Mrs. Arianna Huffington, in which Ms. MacLaine worships Ms. MacLaine (with some justification) and Mrs. Huffington reveres Mrs. Huffington (with perhaps less). There have of course been major Gnostic ecstatics, such as the Shi'ite Sufi Al-Hallaj, who was executed in Baghdad in 922, supposedly for his grand outcry: "I am the Absolute Truth!" But mere Gnosticism, as I conceive it, is rather more modest, and can be less ecstatically conveyed. Return again to your own earliest memories, not of your contexts nor of your empirical self, but of your deeper self, your sense of your own individuality. What I recall must be close enough to what many others doubtless recall: a kind of awakening in which both the world and the self seemed more attuned to one another, so much so that appearances took on a kind of radiance, though only for a time. Transcendental experience of this kind can be reduced by psychoanalysis, or by other modes of explaining things away, but why should we feel obliged to reduce? The reductive fallacy is best exemplified by those persons (we all know them) who ask us the question concerning someone to whom we are close: "But tell me what he or she is *really* like." We tell them, and they reply: "No, I mean *really* like," and we suddenly understand them to mean: "What is the very *worst* thing you can say about him or her that is true, or true enough?" No manifestation of the human spirit could survive that kind of reductiveness.

These days, in the United States, we live surrounded by a religiosity that pervades our politics, media, even our sports events. Kierkegaard fiercely insisted on the difficulty, the near impossibility of "becoming a Christian" in what purported to be a Christian society. What Speaker Gingrich denounces and the *New York Times* defends as "counterculture" essentially is a diffuse religiosity, heretical more in its implications than in its overt affirmations. The New Age, an endlessly entertaining saturnalia of ill-defined yearnings, is less a product of counterculture than it initially seems to be; its origins are in an old mixture of occultism and an American Harmonial faith suspended about halfway between feeling good and good feeling. Rock music, the authentic mark or banner of counterculture, is something that once was a new variety of indigenous American religion, however brief or secular, momentarily akin to the outflarings that have engendered permanent beliefs among us: Mormonism, Pentecostalism, Adventism. The moment passed, probably in the winter of 1969–1970, when spiritual intensity was at a brief height, and when some of my most sensitive students would assure me that the Jefferson Airplane, in concert, provided them with a mystical experience. Doubtless it did, since they attended in high condition, heirs to what William James, in *The Varieties of Religious Experience,* called the "Anesthetic Revelation," provided for the pragmatic philosopher-psychologist by nitrous oxide. The sorrow of the Anesthetic Revelation is that the music stops, the drug wears off, and there is no spiritual aftermath, or at least no awareness that can be put into words. That however is preferable to New Age prose, which is of a vacuity not to be believed.

A transcendence that cannot somehow be expressed is an incoherence; authentic transcendence can be communicated by mastery of language, since metaphor is a transference, a carrying-across from one kind of experience to another. The failure of rock criticism, except of a purely technical sort, is another indication of the retreat from intelligence in the purported counterculture. But my own profession, literary criticism, is currently even more of a failure. Literary experience necessarily has its own relation to transcendence, but who could know that from what now calls itself "cultural criticism," for which there are no selves, whether in writers or readers, but only politics: gender, racial, class, ethnic. Since my own version of self-reliance would be impossible without a sense of the deep self, and since transcendence for me began with the wonder of reading great poetry, I am compelled to testify that literary works can communicate transcendence.

What, very strictly, is transcendence? As an attribute of God, it means a climbing beyond the material universe and ourselves, insofar as we are nothing but units of that universe. As a human attribute, it is dismissed as an illusion by materialists, yet it has an uneasy existence in many of us, and a more secure hold in a scattering of individuals through the ages: mystics, visionaries, sages, men and women who have a direct encounter with the divine or the angelic world and are able to convey something crucial in that encounter to us. Aldous Huxley, introducing his beautiful anthology, *The Perennial Philosophy* (1945), observed that

> . . . it contains but few extracts from the writings of professional men of letters and, though illustrating a philosophy, hardly anything from the professional philosophers. The reason for this is very simple. The Perennial Philosophy is primarily concerned with the one, divine Reality substantial to the manifold world of things and lives and minds. But the nature of this one Reality is such that it cannot be directly and immediately apprehended except by those who have chosen to fulfill certain conditions, making themselves loving, pure in heart, and poor in spirit. Why should this be so? We do not know.

Huxley's principle means that Saint John of the Cross and Meister Eckhart make their way into his book, while Dante, Emerson, and Kierkegaard do not. Neither does William Blake nor any of the great Gnostic speculators, whether the Christian Gnostic Valentinus, or the Muslim Sufi Ibn 'Arabi, or the Jewish Kabbalist Isaac Luria. Self-abnegating spirituality has an ancient and honorable lineage, and always has been compatible with dogmatic orthodoxy in all the Western religions. Self-affirming spirituality has a lineage at least as ancient and as honorable, and has never been reconcilable with institutional and historicized faith. I think it no accident that the spirituality of the strong self has close affiliations with the visions of poets and people-of-letters, so much so that Gnostic and literary writings could and should be gathered together in an anthology that would rival Huxley's fine *The Perennial Philosophy*. Such a book might be called *The Spiritual Arsenal,* because its authors are as aggressive as they can be loving, are divided in heart, and are rich in spirit. Why should this be so? We do know, because the issue precisely *is* knowing. Gnostics, poets, people-of-letters share in the realization of knowing that they know. That brings me to the crucial distinction between Gnosis and Gnosticism, a pragmatic difference that underlies my own experiential path to mere Gnosticism.

3.

C. S. Lewis, concluding one of my least favorite books, *Mere Christianity* (revised edition, 1952), shrewdly associates the Christian surrender of the self with *not* seeking literary originality:

> Until you have given up your self to Him you will not have a real self. . . . Even in literature and art, no man who bothers about originality will ever be original: whereas if you simply try to tell the truth (without caring twopence how often it has been told before) you will, nine times out of ten, become original without ever having noticed it. The principle runs through all life from top to bottom. Give up your self, and you will find your real self. Lose your life and you will save it. Submit to death, death of your ambitions and favourite wishes every day and death of your whole body in the end: submit with every fibre of your being, and you will find eternal life. Keep back nothing. Nothing that you have not given away will ever be really yours. Nothing in you that has not died will ever be raised from the dead. Look for yourself, and you will find in the long run only hatred, loneliness, despair, rage, ruin, and decay. . . .

Setting aside all questions of merely personal distaste, I am fascinated by this passage, because it is the point-by-point reversal of the program of knowing the deep self that is the Gnostic (and literary) quest for immortality. Gnosis depends upon distinguishing the *psyche*, or soul, from the deep self, which pragmatically means that any strengthening of the psy-

deep self — reincarnated ? =

che depends upon acquaintance with the original self, already one with God. Originality is as much the mark of historical Gnosticism as it is of canonical Western literature; that Lewis simultaneously deprecates both the self and originality confirms the Gnostic negative analysis of those who assert that they live by faith rather than by knowledge. Christian "faith" is *pistis,* a believing that something was, is, and will be so. Judaic "faith" is *emunah,* a trusting in the Covenant. *Islam* means "submission" to the will of Allah, as expressed through his messenger Muhammad, "the seal of the prophets." But Gnosis is not a believing that, a trusting in, or a submission. Rather, it is a mutual knowing, and a simultaneous being known, of and by God.

I cannot pretend that this is a simple process; it is far more elitist than C. S. Lewis's "mere Christianity," and I suspect that this elitism is why Gnosticism always has been defeated by orthodox Christian faith, in history. But I am writing spiritual autobiography, and not Gnostic theology, and so I return to personal history to explain how I understand Gnosis and Gnosticism. You don't have to be Jewish to be oppressed by the enormity of the German slaughter of European Jewry, but if you have lost your four grandparents and most of your uncles, aunts, and cousins in the Holocaust, then you will be a touch more sensitive to the normative Judaic, Christian, and Muslim teachings that God is both all-powerful and benign. That gives one a God who tolerated the Holocaust, and such a God is simply intolerable, since he must be either crazy or irresponsible if his benign omnipotence was compatible with the death camps. A cosmos this obscene, a nature that contains schizophrenia, is acceptable to the monotheistic orthodox as part of "the mystery of faith." Historical Gnosticism, so far as I can surmise, was invented by the Jews of the first century of the Common Era as a protest against just such a mystery of faith which, as Emily Dickinson wrote, "bleats to understand." Yet "Gnosticism" is an ambiguous term; even "the Gnostic religion," Hans Jonas's suggestion, creates difficulties, as he acknowledged. There were, so far as we can ascertain, few, perhaps no Gnostic churches or temples in the ancient world. And yet Gnosticism was more than a tendency, more even than a party or a movement: I think it is best to call it a spirituality, one that was and is a deliberate, strong revision of Judaism and Christianity, and of Islam later. There is a quality of unprecedentedness about Gnosticism, an atmosphere of originality that disconcerts the orthodox of any faith. Creativity and imagination, irrelevant and even dangerous to dogmatic religion, are essential to Gnosticism. When I encounter this quality, I recognize it instantly, and an answering, cognitive music responds in me.

4.

In the middle of the journey, at thirty-five, now thirty years ago, I got very wretched, and for almost a year was immersed in acute melancholia. Colors faded away, I could not read, and scarcely could look up at the sky. Teaching, my most characteristic activity, became impossible to perform. Whatever the immediate cause of my depression had been, that soon faded away in irrelevance, and I came to sense that my crisis was spiritual. An enormous vastation had removed the self, which until then had seemed strong in me. At the suggestion of my Yale psychiatrist, I went abroad, but found myself so depressed in London that I went to sec an eminent Pakistani psychoanalyst, at my Yale doctor's recommendation. An instant hatred sprang up between the London analyst and me, so that I refused to see him again after three visits, but my fury was therapeutic and partly dislodged me from my dark night of the soul. I tell this story only because the dislodgment was, at first, so very partial. What rescued me, back in 1965, was a process that began as reading, and then became a kind of "religious" conversion that was also an excursion into a personal literary theory. I had purchased *The Gnostic Religion* by Hans Jonas when it was published as a paperback in 1963, and had first read it then, assimilating it to William Blake, upon whom I was writing commentaries, and to Gershom Scholem's studies of Kabbalah. But Jonas's book had a delayed impact upon me; it did not kindle until I began to read endlessly in all of Emerson, throughout 1965-66. I still remember the passages in Emerson that retrospectively linked up with Jonas, in my mind:

> That is always best which gives me to myself. The sublime is excited in me by the great stoical doctrine, Obey thyself. That which shows God in me, fortifies me. That which shows God out of me, makes me a wart and a wen. . . .

> In the highest moments, we are a vision. There is nothing that can be called gratitude nor properly joy. The soul is raised over passion. It seeth nothing so much as Identity. It is

a Perceiving that Truth and Right ARE. Hence it becomes a perfect Peace out of the knowing that all things will go well. Vast spaces of nature, the Atlantic Ocean, the South Sea; vast intervals of time, years, centuries, are annihilated to it; this which I think and feel underlay that former state of life and circumstances, as it does underlie my present, and will always all circumstance, and what is called life and what is called death.

. . . Those men who cannot answer by a superior wisdom these facts or questions of time, serve them. Facts encumber them, tyrannize over them, and make the men of routine, the men of *sense*, in whom a literal obedience to facts has extinguished every spark of that light by which man is truly man. . . .

For Jonas, as for Emerson, the moment of *Gnosis* is the mind's direct perception, a pure movement and event that simultaneously discloses a divine spark in the self, and a sense of divine degradation even there, in the inmost self, because the Gnostic Fall is *within* the Godhead. What integrating Jonas and Emerson did for me was to find the context for my nihilistic depression. Jonas gives a catalog of affects that accompany the Gnostic sense of *having been thrown* into this existence: forlornness, dread, homesickness, numbness, sleep, intoxication. The transcendent stranger God or alien God of Gnosticism, being beyond our cosmos, is no longer an effective force; God exists, but is so hidden that he has become a nihilistic conception, in himself. He is not responsible for our world of death camps and schizophrenia, but he is so estranged and exiled that he is powerless. We are unsponsored, since the God of this world, wor-shipped (as Blake said) by the names of Jesus and Jehovah, is only a bungler, an archangel-artisan who botched the False Cre-ation that we know as our Fall.

As Americans, we are now post-pragmatists; we acknowl-edge only differences that make a difference. It makes a con-siderable difference to believe that you go back before the Creation; that you were always there, a part and particle of God. Self-reliance is a solitary doctrine; it disagrees strongly with Marx's contention that the smallest human unit is two peo-ple. Mere Gnosticism does not lend itself to communal worship, though doubtless that has been ventured, at one time and place or another. What should a Gnostic prayer be? A call to the self, perhaps, to wake up, in order to be made free by the Gnosis. Emerson, American prophet, says it for us: "That is always best which gives me to myself."

5.

We live now, more than ever, in an America where a great many people are Gnostics without knowing it, which is a peculiar irony. When Newt Gingrich tells us that our national economic future depends completely upon information, then I recall that the ancient Gnostics denied both matter and energy, and opted instead for information above all else. Gnostic information has two primary awarenesses: first, the estrangement, even the alienation of God, who has abandoned this cosmos, and second, the location of a residuum of divinity in the Gnostic's own inmost self. That deepest self is no part of nature, or of history: it is devoid of matter or energy, and so is not part of the Creation-Fall, which for a Gnostic constitutes one and the same event. If Gingrich is an unknowing American right-wing Gnostic, we abound also in a multitude of unaware left-wing Gnostics, who like Gingrich seek salvation through rather different information. Gingrich is much under the influence of the future-shock maven, Alvin Toffler, whose vision of a New America is not coherent enough for me to apprehend, except that the way to apotheosis lies through ever more advanced information technology. I myself, in an ironic moment, once characterized ancient Gnosticism as an information theory, but I little realized that every possible parody, even of Gnosticism, would be available all around us in our Gingrichian nation. Enemies of Gnosticism have confounded it with every kind of modern ideology, yet its supposed friends do it more damage. Our current angel worship in America is another debased parody of Gnosticism, though here I will have to go rather a long way back to explain how curious our angelic rage truly is, and why it is here to stay, at least until we are into the twenty-first century.

There are angels throughout the Hebrew Bible but they rarely are central concerns, and frequently they are editorial revisions, surrogates for Yahweh whenever the priestly redactors felt the early J writer was being too daring in the depiction of God. Angels become dominant figures, replacing an increasingly remote God, only in the apocalyptic writings of the Jews in the third and second centuries before the Common Era, in a Palestine under the rule of the Hellenistic successors of Alexander the Great. Indeed, angels were not a Jewish invention, but truly returned from Babylonian captivity with the Jews. Their ultimate source is the angelology of Zoroastrian Persia, which may go back as far as 1500 B.C.E. Zoroaster (the Greek form of his actual name, Zarathustra, which was much preferred by Nietzsche) is a shadowy figure for most of us, but he seems to have invented our religiously based sense of apocalypse and Millennium, ideas that did not exist before him. Sometimes curiously refracted, Zoroaster's original ideas reappeared in late apocalyptic Judaism, in Gnosticism, and in early Christianity, and surfaced again in the Shi'ite branch of Islam, which dominates Iran until this day. The scholar Norman Cohn, our great authority upon the Millennium, recently has argued that what binds together post-biblical Jewish apocalypses like the Books of Enoch and some of the Dead Sea Scrolls, as well as the New Testament, is the Zoroastrian vision, which posits a dualistic struggle between supernatural forces of good and evil, a struggle ending with good triumphant, and the Kingdom of God established upon earth. Such doctrines as the existence of the Devil and the other fallen angels, and the resurrection of the dead, besides the entire world of supportive angelology, seem to be Jewish, Christian, and finally Muslim importations from Zoroaster's Iranian spirituality. The ironies of such an inheritance are palpable, and are particularly accented right now, when the doomsday scenarios of informed American and Israeli analysts emphasize the threat of Iran acquiring its own atomic bombs within five years, just in time to greet the Millennium with hellfire. The fall of the Soviet Union into another wretchedly imperial Russia has deprived our American Protestant diviners, like the Reverend Pat Robertson, of an apocalyptic rough beast, which the Iranian juggernaut now can replace. American Christian Fundamentalism, and the Islamic Shi'ite fundamentalism of Iran, are rival heirs of the Zoroastrian imaginings of the Last Things. Norman Cohn points out that the Book of Daniel's symbolism of four metals representing the four ages of the world culminates in the fourth and last age (ours) being symbolized by "iron mixed with [Adam's] clay," a direct borrowing from a Zoroastrian apocalyptic work.

But what has all this to do with Gnosticism, or with anyone's personal Gnosis, such as my own? Gnosticism, then and now, in my judgment rises as a protest against apocalyptic faith, even when it rises within such a faith, as it did successively within Judaism, Christianity, and Islam. Prophetic religion becomes apocalyptic when prophecy fails, and apocalyptic religion becomes Gnosticism when apocalypse fails, as fortunately it always has and, as we must hope, will fail again. Gnosticism does not fail; it cannot fail, because its God is at once deep within the self and also estranged, infinitely far off, beyond our cosmos. Historically, Gnosticism has always been obliterated by persecution, ranging from the relatively benign rejections of normative Judaism through the horrible violence of Roman Catholicism against the Christian Gnostics throughout the ages, wherever and whenever the Church has been near allied to repressive secular authorities. The final organized Western Gnosticism was destroyed in the so-called Albigensian Crusades, which devastated southern France in the thirteenth century, exterminating not only the Cathar Gnostic heretics but also the Provençal language and its troubador culture, which has survived only in the prevalent Western myth and ideal of romantic love. It is yet another irony that our erotic lives, with their self-destructive reliance upon the psychic disease called "falling—or being—in love," should be a final, unknowing heritage of the last organized Gnosticism to date.

I need to modify or amend that, since Gnosticism is alive and well (perhaps not so well) in our America, and not just in New Age parodies, though I am delighted to be told by the *New York Times* that Speaker Newt keeps Arianna Huffington's treatise, *The Fourth Instinct*, in his office bookcase. Most intrepid of readers, I have attempted it, only to be driven back in defeat by its inspired vacuity. Our authentic Gnosticisms are scattered wherever our new southern and western Republican overlords worship: in Salt Lake City and Dallas and wherever else Mormon temples and Southern Baptist First Churches pierce the heavens. Our American Religion, whether homegrown or ostensibly Roman Catholic and mainline Protestant, is more of a Gnostic amalgam than a European kind of historical and doctrinal Christianity, though very few are able to see this, or perhaps most don't wish to see it. Some alarmed Catholic priests trying to hold on against the angry feminists of Woman Church—a fierce, huge coven that threatens to seize the church in many places—have become aware of their danger, and there are a handful or so of mainline Protestant ministers who now understand that their neo-orthodoxy is yielding to a populist neo-Gnosticism. But the major manifestations transcend the churches, and are far larger than even the legions of New Age fellow travelers. Our rampantly flourishing industries of angel worship, "near-death experiences," and astrology—dream divination networks—are the mass versions of an adulterated or travestied Gnosticism. I sometimes allow myself the fantasy of Saint Paul redescending upon a contemporary America where he still commands extraordinary honor, among religions as diverse as Roman Catholicism and Southern Baptism. He would be bewildered, not by change, but by sameness, and would believe he was back at Corinth and Colossae, confronted again by Gnostic myths of the angels who made this world. If you read Saint Paul, you discover that he was no friend of the angels. There is his cryptic remark in 1 Corinthians 11:10 that "a woman ought to have a veil on her head, because of the angels," which I suspect goes back to the Book of Enoch's accounts of angelic lust for earthly women. In the Letter to the Colossians, the distinction between angels and demons seems to be voided, and Christians are warned against "worship of angels," an admonition that the churches, at the moment, seem afraid to restate.

The "near-death experience" is another pre-Millennium phenomenon that travesties Gnosticism; every account we are given of this curious matter culminates in being "embraced by the light," by a figure of light known to Gnostic tradition variously as "the astral body," "the Resurrection Body," or Hermes, our guide in the land of the dead. Since all of life is, in a sense, a "near-death experience," it does seem rather odd that actual cases of what appear to be maldiagnoses should become supposed intimations of immortality. The commercialization of angelology and of out-of-the-body shenanigans properly joins the age-old history of mercantilized astrology and dream divination. As mass-audience omens of Millennium, all of these represent what may be the final debasement of a populist American Gnosticism. I am prompted by this to go back to the great texts of a purer Gnosticism and their best commentators.

The anarchistic Brethren of the Free Spirit in the fifteenth century, like the Provençal Cathars in the twelfth, join the Manichaeans as the three large instances of Gnostic movements that transcended an esoteric religion of the intellectuals. Ancient Gnosticism, like Romantic and modern varieties, was a religion of the elite only, almost a literary religion. A purified Gnosticism, then and now, is truly for a relative handful only, and perhaps is as much an aesthetic as it is a spiritual discipline. But, as the Millennium approaches, with the remote yet real possibility of a virtual Gingrichian America, we may behold a mass Gnosticism of protest rise out of a new Brethren of the Free Spirit, compounded of an urban dispossessed without federal welfare, and the sorry legions of Generation X, the middle-class young who will resent laboring all their lives to pay off the deficits of the Reaganite and Gingrichian revolutions. It is a dismal prophecy, but 1996–2004 *could* continue to be the reign of Speaker Gingrich, and thus become a future shock indeed, a Christian Coalition (with some Jewish neoconservative camp followers) that could repeal much of the Bill of Rights through constitutional amendments, while returning us to the America of the late nineteenth-century robber barons.

Envision a United States of Virtual Gingrichia paying for its balanced budget with a high national sales tax, burdensome in particular upon the poor, black and white. With institutional Christianity—whether mainline Protestant, Roman Catholic, or American sectarian (Southern Baptist and Mormon in particular)—part and parcel of the Gingrichian Establishment, we might see a Gnostic heresy rise up as a mass movement among the exploited, perhaps even pulling Pentecostalism away from its present reactionary alliances. An America of welfare riots, of an enforced contractual Gingrichian Virtual Gospel, founded upon an informational monopoly, might well provoke a large-scale Gnosticism of the insulted and injured, rising up to affirm and defend the divine spark in themselves. If an unregenerate Gingrich triumphs, then the only self-reliance left to the dispossessed might be a religiously inspired resistance. Like everyone else, I would like to dismiss all that as mere fantasy, rather than as future-shock mere Gnosticism.

CHAPTER I

NGELS

VISIONS OF ANGELS

ngels are anything but ephemeral images. The historical sequence of Western religions—Zoroastrianism, Judaism, Christianity, Islam—has not known how to tell the story of their truths without angelic intercessions, nor is there any major religious tradition, Eastern or Western, that does not rely upon angels. The spiritual life, whether expressed in worship and prayer, in private contemplation, or in the arts, needs some kind of vision of the angels. That vision burgeons in some eras and falls away in others, yet on some level it generally abides. Even secularists and metaphysical materialists are likely to speak of someone's good angel or her bad angel, but rarely is it said that the angel of morning or of evening is at hand. Partly this is because even believers frequently regard angels as ambiguous beings: are they purely spirits or do they have bodies, do they eat and drink, do they make love and war? Saint Augustine himself, greatest of all Christian authorities, said that we did not know whether angels had material bodies, but this wise remark was not influential. Saint Thomas Aquinas can be taken to represent the Scholastic Catholic position that angels are purely spiritual, while the poet John Milton can stand for all those humanists and Protestants who insisted that all actual beings must be embodied. Milton, in the major work of all Western angelology, his epic poem *Paradise Lost*, emphasizes that his angels eat and digest human food, make love to other angels, and can be wounded (but not slain) in combat with their own kind. His good angels are also heretical in that they stand by their own strength, not God's grace, and thus resemble the Miltonic exaltation of man, who must also stand or fall upon the power of his own free will. The most extraordinary portrait of any angel that ever we have had or will have is of Milton's Satan, who employs his freedom to damn himself titanically.

Robert H. West, in his *Milton and the Angels* (1955), emphasizes that the poet's great originality, a break with all previous Christian angelologists, was to insist that angels, unfallen and fallen, made love to one another for the pleasure of fulfillment, and not to beget angelic offspring. There was a long tradition, Zoroastrian and Jewish apocryphal, that many of the angels fell out of lust for the fair daughters of men, but John Milton seems to have had no Christian precedent for his amiable assumption that angels lusted for one another, and did something about it. There were Kabbalist and other esoteric sources available for angelic sexuality, yet Milton seems to have had no real knowledge of these. His angels are alternately male and female, exchanging genders with their sexual partners, somewhat in the mode of human sexuality on the planet Gether or Winter, in Ursula K. Le Guin's wonderful fantasy novel *The Left Hand of Darkness*. Though the Bible's angels, like the Koran's, appear to be males only, the older tradition in Persia and Babylonia stressed the existence of female angels also, an emphasis that reappears in rabbinical lore and that achieves amplification in the Kabbalah. Milton, very much a sect of one, makes his angels very human, and his Adam and Eve highly angelic, so as to exalt again the image of the human, and in particular to celebrate the divine possibilities implicit in human sexuality.

For Milton, angels were a mirror into which all of us gaze, and behold neither ourselves nor an absolute otherness, but a middle region where self and other mingle. Jakob Boehme, the German Protestant mystic of the late sixteenth and early seventeenth centuries, gazed into the angelic mirror and saw a blending very different from what Milton was to see. Boehme's angels, who are God's thoughts, are shaped like humans, being wingless, and they have hands and feet, but their mouths have no teeth, since they eat only the fruit of Paradise. These Germanic angels are not mere messengers; God cannot rule nature or human nature without them since they are his only instruments. If they all defected at once, then Boehme's God would be pragmatically powerless, because the positive and negative elements that make up God's dual nature would reach a permanent standstill, and the angels reinforce the positive side. A century after Boehme, another formidable mystic, Emanuel

Swedenborg, had a more comprehensive vision of the angels. All of the Swedenborgian angels were once mortal and human: the angel is therefore the form of the resurrection. Himself a distinguished mining engineer, Swedenborg regarded the angelic mirror and discovered therein a Heaven and Hell, which he described in minute detail, rather as if he were conducting a survey of foreign mineral rights. So vast and sublimely literalistic is Swedenborg's report that the reader soon feels that both Heaven and Hell are countries best left unvisited, even though conjugal love flourishes in the angelic world, so that fresh marriages are made there. What is oddest about the Swedenborgian angels is that they are not odd at all; they are as banal as your neighbors. The English poet William Blake, who was born in 1757, the year that Swedenborg called the Last Judgment in the spiritual world, cheerfully satirized Swedenborg's angels. In Blake these angels are time-serving upholders of the Enlightenment's threefold exaltation of reason, nature, and society, and so are proper targets of the satirist's art.

After Blake, the angels seemed to withdraw, except for a solitary visionary like the young Joseph Smith, founder of Mormonism. There are angels aplenty in nineteenth- and twentieth-century art and literature, but they tend to be isolated and idiosyncratic images of a lost spirituality. And yet they remain a mirror of spiritual aspiration, perhaps more a study of the nostalgias of belief than a manifestation of faith in their own splendor. That there is a human longing for angels, perpetual and unappeasable on the part of many, is beyond denial. A desire for the consolations of a spiritual life transcends institutional, historical, and dogmatic structures, and belongs to human nature itself. The image of the angel appears to many of us in what seem to be prophetically troubling dreams, or it hovers at crisis moments of near death as the shape of an astral body. All the centuries have their burdens of catastrophe; only a few match the terrors of the one now expiring. We may expect angels as omens of the Millennium, just as we may be prepared to encounter them at the gates of the dream, or on the threshold of death.

Millennium, or the advent of a messianic age (in the expectations of some among us), arouses inevitably ambivalent sensations even in those who scoff at the arbitrariness of arithmetic that governs such calculations. Our ultimate heritage from Zoroaster, the prophet of the oldest monotheism still extant, in just a few in Iran and a small number in India, is our sense of a possible end-time. Before Zoroaster, all religions envisioned time as being cyclic, perpetually to return upon itself. From Zoroaster on, apocalyptic expectations flourished and made their way into Judaism and its heretical child, early Christianity, and then into Islam, which sprang forth from Jewish Christianity. Zoroaster is the ultimate ancestor of the Millennium, even as his angelology initially engendered the angels who came to throng Judaism, Christianity, and Islam. I find it fitting that Iranian Islam, among the Shi'ite Sufis, created the most persuasive account of the angelic realm, by drawing directly upon the imaginative heritage of the religion of the Iranian prophet Zoroaster. The universe of the angels found its strongest theoreticians in the Sufis, as I will demonstrate later.

THEIR CURRENT DEBASEMENT

Polls, which are very American, tell us that sixty-nine percent of us believe in angels, while only twenty-five percent of us do not. Forty-six percent among us have their own guardian angels; twenty-one percent deny that anyone has a guardian angel. We are rather more divided on the nature of the angels: fifty-five percent say that angels are higher beings created by God as his agents, but fifteen percent identify them as the spirits of the dead. Eighteen percent reduce angels to mere religious symbols, and seven percent insist that angels are nonsense. Experientially, thirty-two percent of Americans have felt angelic presence, just short of the thirty-five percent who have not. There is a falling-off from the sixty-nine percent who believe in angels or devils as against forty-five percent who dissent. I suspect that there is a near identity between the sixty-seven percent of Americans who believe in life after death and the sixty-nine percent who are devoted to the angels, since the two beliefs reinforce one another. But only (only!) fifteen percent report a "near-death experience," less than half of those who have known the reality of angelic presence. These figures, while perhaps surprising to some secular intellectuals, are quite consistent with a nation of believers, where nearly nine out of ten affirm that God loves them on a personal and individual basis. If we remember, as we should, that the United States always has seen itself as the millennial nation, both before and after the American Revolution, then our preoccupation with such phenomena as angelic visitations, visionary dreams, and astral-body appearances in "near-death experience" will seem to be altogether normative.

Angels, these days, have been divested of their sublimity by popular culture. It may be that the domestication of angels, which by now has reduced them to being easy, and therefore vulgar, actually began with their aesthetic humanization by the painters of the Italian Renaissance. One can predict that angels will be at least partly restored to their equivocal glory as the Millennium nears, and a more accurate interest replaces a diffused enthusiasm. Even in the Hebrew Bible, there are equivocal elements and ambiguities in the angels: how could there not be, since they serve or substitute for Yahweh, and he is, in the original J text, an ambivalent, uncanny, and unpredictable personality, given to violent mood swings.

Are we only a parody of the angels? Or were we created to supplant them? In a fragment of Valentinus, the most imaginative of the Gnostic heresiarchs, we are told that the angels were terrified when they gazed at the unfallen Adam, and in that terror they spoiled their creation of our world. As we drift towards Millennium, angels haunt us, on every level, from popular culture through Tony Kushner's *Angels in America* and Jose Rivera's *Marisol* on to James Merrill's epic poem, *The Changing Light at Sandover*. Such hauntings, even on stage, sometimes make angels into playthings. Our prevalent symptom of belatedness is the decline of intellectual standards: in government, in universities, in media, in the arts. Our angels reflect this decline; in our New Age, the upper spheres, where the angels live, are overpopulated, so that even the least deserving of us can be assigned a guardian messenger. The rage for angelic protection, while more than American, has become peculiarly acute in the United States, where constantly I walk by people in the streets who wear cherub pins. Whatever original purpose the angels served, their prime enterprise now seems to be reassuring Americans, only a few years before the coming Millennium. If there is an overarching Angel of America, he or she is not yet named, except perhaps for Mormons, and for only a few others besides.

Our passion for angels is not surprising in a nation where one of the ongoing mottoes is "God's country and mine!" If God loves us individually, then it follows that most of us should have an angel of her or his own. To find your angel is not necessarily to find yourself, though most quests for the angels seem nowadays to suppose that a guardian angel is rather more like a dog or a cat than like a husband or a wife. You acquire an angel in the expectation that this addition to your household will give you perpetual and unconditional love. Questing for resurrection, we turn to ancient figures, to ideas of order that may aid in stabilizing an anxious time, which will extend itself at least until Millennium, the advent of the year 2001.

METATRON, WHO WAS ENOCH

Angels once were more ambiguous and ambivalent, and traditionally their roles have not always been comforting or protective in regard to us. But they suit us now for many reasons, particularly because, like us, they suffer from (and represent) a condition of belatedness: they are not originary beings. They barely make their way into the Hebrew Bible: almost never by name, and I have noted that frequently they are a redactor's substitutes for daringly human appearances by God himself, Yahweh in the earliest stratum of biblical text.

The pre-exilic Bible is very much the Book of David the King, who subtly dominates the early Yahwistic text, where however he is never mentioned, since it embraces history from the Creation through the entry into Canaan. The court of David essentially was a military society, with the hero-king presiding over his mighty men and an admonitory prophet or two. In the ensuing age of Solomon, a highly cultivated court surrounded the monarch, who administered a commercial society, urbanized and relatively at peace, but still locating its ideal in the charismatic David. Whatever his actual power, Solomon does not seem to have adopted the full panoply of ancient Near Eastern despotism, with all its hierarchal bureaucracies. But in Babylon the Jews beheld what must have been an immense and elaborate royal court, whose structure mirrored the supposed hierarchy of the heavens. God, after the Babylonian exile, reigns over a cosmos of angelic orders, and is no longer the solitary warrior-god, Yahweh, who employed a handful of the Elohim as his messengers and agents. Out of Babylon came not only angelic names but angel-bureaucrats, princes, and functionaries.

Jewish legends clustered about the idea that the angels had been made on the second day of creation rather than on the first. Implicit in these legends is a polemic against Jewish Gnostic heretics, who wished to attribute the creation to the angels rather than to God, thus insinuating a flaw at the origins. What seems clear is that there can be no definitive or exemplary account of the angels. Shadowy in the biblical text, they emerge most starkly in post-biblical days and haunt the time of troubles that was the matrix of Christianity. The apocalyptic literature of roughly 200 B.C.E. to 200 C.E. is the true domain of the angels, and is associated with Enoch. Enoch, a mysterious patriarch of whom we are told only that he "walked with God, and then was not, because God took him," is the single most crucial figure in the long history of the angels, even though he began existence as a man. After God took him, Enoch became an extraordinary angel, perhaps more a god than an angel, because frequently he was called "the lesser Yahweh." This god-angel, Metatron, sets the pattern for ascents to Heaven by Jacob (first as Uriel, then as Israel), and by Elijah, who became the angel Sandalphon. Saint Francis, according to some of his followers, enjoyed a similar transformation. Perhaps Dante's Beatrice could be considered a fifth in this remarkable company except that, for her poet, she evidently already was an angel as a young girl, and required no apotheosis. Enoch-Metatron, I will suggest later in this book, may be regarded as the authentic angel of America, which was initially the insight of the Mormon prophet, seer, and revelator Joseph Smith, who identified himself with Enoch, and by now may well be joined in an imaginative unity with his great precursor, if Mormon speculation proves true.

What we now refer to as 1 Enoch is preserved completely only in the ancient Ethiopic language, but fragments discovered among the Dead Sea Scrolls demonstrate that the book's original language was Aramaic, which was spoken by the Jews as by neighboring Syriac peoples for several centuries before and after the start of the Common Era. Aramaic, by some traditions, is the language of the angels, which makes it appropriate that 1 Enoch should have been composed in that tongue (though other traditions insist that angels speak only Hebrew).

1 Enoch is a savage reading experience, best available now in the translation by E. Isaac in *The Old Testament Pseud-epigrapha: Apocalyptic Literature and Testaments,* edited by James H. Charlesworth (1983). In a remarkable expansion of Genesis 6:1–4, the author of 1 Enoch begins with the descent of some two hundred lustful angels, who come down upon the summit of Mount Hermon in pursuit of the beautiful daughters of men. They are led by Semyaz, later the Greek Orion, thus perpetually punished as an upside-down figure. After mating with earthly women, the fallen angels raise up giant sons of voracious appetite, who successively devour produce, beasts, people, and one another.

Contemplating this horror, and the dreadful teaching of magic and witchcraft by Azaz'el, one of the demons, God sends a deluge upon earth, and orders the archangel Raphael to bury Azaz'el under the stones of the wilderness. At just this point, Enoch the righteous scribe enters the narrative. In a dream vision, the Watchers, or angels, send Enoch to reprimand and warn the fallen angels of what awaits them. But first Enoch ascends to the throne of God, in a region of fire, and is allowed to confront God. A series of heavenly journeys follows, a kind of tour of the angelic realms, and of all the secrets of the cosmos. These include an epiphany of a messianic son of the people (perhaps misleadingly translated by Isaac with the now Christian overtone of "Son of Man"), as well as tableaux of the resurrection of the dead and the final judgment of the sinners.

The Ethiopic Enoch, for all its vividness, is dwarfed by the apocalyptic splendor and rigors of 3 Enoch, a work written in Hebrew probably in the fifth century C.E., and brilliantly translated by P. Alexander in the Charlesworth *Pseudepigrapha*. This rhapsodic vision purports to be the work of the great rabbi Ishmael, slain by the Romans as one of the preludes to Bar Kokhba's insurrection in 132 C.E., but undoubtedly the date of composition is much later. As an apocalypse, 3 Enoch belongs to the pre-Kabbalistic tradition of Hebraic gnosis called *Merkabah* mysticism, the *Merkabah* being the prophet Ezekiel's term for the chariot that bears the Enthroned Man of his vision. In this tradition, the visionary voyages through the heavenly halls until he comes upon the throne of God, where a revelation is vouchsafed to him. And yet, since we are within the normative rabbinical world, the revelation is severely restricted; the exuberant invention of Gnostic writing would be a violation of decorum and of received scriptural authority.

It is surprising how much mythopoeic invention gets into 3 Enoch anyway, perhaps because we are at an early stage of what will develop, half a millennium later, into the extravagant Kabbalistic imagination. At the imagistic center of 3 Enoch is the radical transformation of Enoch into the archangel Metatron, Prince of the Divine Presence (a title from the prophet Isaiah) and a kind of viceroy for Yahweh himself. In this transmutation, Enoch's skin is replaced by a fiery Garment of Light, and his human dimensions expand to the length and breadth of the created world. Moshe Idel, the leading contemporary scholar of Kabbalah, shrewdly observes that Enoch's apotheosis is the point-for-point reversal of the collapse of "the supernal Adam" into the Adam of Genesis, since ancient Jewish texts, both normative and heterodox, initially represented Adam as a god-man whose Garment of Light is replaced by his own skin and the animal skins in which God clothes him, while the primordial giant Adam, whose size and splendor awed and frightened the angels, dwindles into our merely human contours. Idel also notes the irony of another reversal: in some sources the primal Adam "falls" because of angelic sin, since his splendor moves the angels to assert that Adam and God are equal powers.

In 3 Enoch, one interpolated passage records the culpability of Elisha ben Abuya, the second-century C.E. colleague of Ishmael and Akiba. Elisha ben Abuya was condemned as heretical by the Talmud for his supposed Gnostic heresies. Confronting Metatron, Acher ("the other"), as Elisha ben Abuya was called by the rabbis, cries out, "There are two Powers in Heaven!" thus condemning Metatron to a divine chastisement. I would expand Idel's insight by suggesting that Metatron is not only the new primordial, supernal Adam, but also that Metatron becomes the esoteric link in angelology between the divine and the human, fusing these realms in the manner of the Iranian "Man of Light," whether Zoroastrian or Sufi. Enoch was renamed Idris by the Koran, and the Sufis identified Idris with the ancient Greek Hermes, remembering that the Hermetic Corpus centered upon the image of Hermes as the Perfect Nature, the union of man and God. Metatron might well be interpreted as the unique angel of *reintegration,* which is why he became the most important of angels for the *Zohar* and for all subsequent Kabbalah. I venture that Metatron is the archangel of our moment as we approach the Millennium; all the omens—other angels, prophetic dreams, manifestations of the Resurrection Body—are aspects of his being. As the lesser Yahweh, he is the angel of angels; he is also the celestial interpreter of prophetic dreams; his transfigured form is the astral body of the "near-death experience"; his man-God reintegration restores the supernal Adam and illuminates the messianic aspects of the Millennium.

In 3 Enoch, Metatron is presented with a certain reticence; the apocalyptic impulse in the text is frequently tempered by a normative censor, reflecting the curious nature of this work, which would appear to have a prolixity of authors, some of them evidently later normative redactors. Hence the startling contrast between successive sections of 3 Enoch, 15 and 16. Here is 15:

R. Ishmael said: The angel Metatron, Prince of the Divine Presence, the glory of highest heaven, said to me:

When the Holy One, blessed be he, took me to serve the throne of glory, the wheels of the chariot and all the needs of the Shekhinah, at once my flesh turned to flame, my sinews to blazing fire, my bones to juniper coals, my eyelashes to lightning flashes, my eyeballs to fiery torches, the hairs of my head to hot flames, all my limbs to wings of burning fire, and the substance of my body to blazing fire. On my right—those who cleave flames of fire—on my left—burning brands—round about me swept wind, tempest, and storm; and the roar of earthquake was before and behind me.

The *Shekhinah,* the feminine element in Yahweh, his indwelling presence in the world, is served by Metatron even as he serves the divine throne and chariot. Since the *Shekhinah* dwells among us, this means that Metatron is the grand vizier of Yahweh on earth even as he is in heaven. The magnificent metamorphosis here of *Enoch,* a mortal man, into the lesser Yahweh contrasts overwhelmingly with the subsequent whipping and dethronement of Metatron through no fault of his own, since he is in no way responsible for the heretical Acher:

R. Ishmael said: The angel Metatron, Prince of the Divine Presence, the glory of highest heaven, said to me:

At first I sat upon a great throne at the door of the seventh palace, and I judged all the denizens of the heights on the authority of the Holy One, blessed be he. I assigned greatness, royalty, rank, sovereignty, glory, praise, diadem, crown, and honor to all the princes of the kingdoms, when I sat in the heavenly court. The princes of kingdoms stood beside me, to my right and to my left, by authority of the Holy One, blessed be he. But when Acher came to behold the vision of the chariot and set eyes upon me, he was afraid and trembled before me. His soul was alarmed to the point of leaving him because of his fear, dread, and terror of me, when he saw me seated upon a throne like a king, with ministering angels standing beside me as servants and all the princes of kingdoms crowned with crowns surrounding me. Then he opened his mouth and said, "There are indeed two powers in heaven!" Immediately a divine voice came out from the presence of the Shekhinah and said, "Come back to me, apostate sons—apart from Acher!" Then Anapi'el YHWH, the honored, glorified, beloved, wonderful, terri-

ble, and dreadful Prince, came at the command of the Holy
One, blessed be he, and struck me with sixty lashes of fire
and made me stand to my feet.

Metatron has his throne at the door of the seventh palace
because 3 Enoch shares with several ancient Gnostic texts the
myth of a heavenly ascent of the soul, in this life in Jewish
works such as 3 Enoch, but after death in Gnostic writings. This
upward journey is always in seven stages, or palaces in the
Merkabah tradition, and yet the journeys are radically different.
In a Gnostic text like *The Hypostasis of the Archons,* the soul is
stopped at each of seven spheres, where a negative spirit, the archon, or ruler of that sphere, would block the aspiring soul, unless it knows and speaks the archon's true name, and shows him
the precisely appropriate seal. In 3 Enoch, the heavens are numbered, but go unnamed, though their ruling angels can be addressed by name. The seven palaces (or temples, or heavens)
are arranged concentrically, and at their center is the *Merkabah,*
the chariot of God that is also his throne. In front of the throne,
a curtain shields the angels from the dangerous radiance of
God, and has embroidered upon it the entire span of history
from Adam to the era of the Messiah. Rivers of fire flow out
from underneath the throne, and the aura of the scene is appro-
priately stark. The angelic gatekeepers are not quite as overtly
hostile as the Gnostic archons, but they certainly are not
friendly. Essentially they are barriers between God and man,
except for the problematical Metatron, who is as protective of
God as the others, but who retains his almost unique status as a

transfigured mortal. The Kabbalistic formula became: "Enoch is Metatron," a shorthand way of implying that the mystic could emulate another human and mount up to the status of the archangel Michael (with whom Metatron sometimes is identified).

As Adam fell, so Enoch was raised, and the demarcation between man and God wavered, and might waver again. For me, the most memorable passage in 3 Enoch comes in section 6, when the angels scorn and protest the apotheosis of Metatron, who was Enoch:

> As soon as I reached the heavenly heights, the holy creatures, the ophanium, the seraphim, the cherubim, the wheels of the chariot and the ministers of consuming fire, smelled my odor 365,000 myriads of parasangs off, they said, "What is this smell of one born of a woman? Why does a white drop ascend on high and serve among those who cleave the flames?"

This is a grand, brief summation of what our current sentimentalization obscures and debases: the profound ambivalence of the angels towards us. The angelic derision is provoked by human sexuality: that "white drop" is the contribution of Jared, his father, to the engendering of Enoch. God's reply to the angels is at once a massive reproof to them and a poignant complaint against us: "This one whom I have taken is my sole reward from my whole world under heaven."

THE CATHOLIC ANGELIC HIERARCHY

Roman Catholic doctrine, as set forth by Saint Thomas Aquinas, argues for the necessity of angels. God did not have to create, but once he had done so, out of his goodness, then angels had to be part of the Creation, for God desires, up to a point, that his creatures should imitate him. Saint Thomas, with customary brilliance, asserts that since God is himself a pure intelligence, then he must create pure intelligences in the angels, since they alone can properly imitate God. Humans, in contrast, can imitate God only in a more limited way. "Pure," for Saint Thomas, is a synonym for spirit: God and the angels alike are free from matter. Here Saint Thomas, though not a party of one, does not necessarily speak for the Church, since other great theologians (Saint Bernard and Saint Bonaventure) have insisted that only God is beyond materiality. And indeed one remembers the angels of Enoch begetting giants upon the daughters of men, and Raphael in the Book of Tobias speaking of his food and drink, and one recalls all of the imagery of fire that pervades descriptions of the angels. Much of the tradition is very different from Saint Thomas, yet it is difficult not to be moved by his passion and his insight when he urges us to consider the angels as pure spirits, as intelligences uncontaminated by bodily drives. God, according to Saint Thomas, made the angels for the sake of his own glory, and the glory of God is beyond matter. It is also beyond enumeration, and so Saint Thomas insists that the sheer numbers of angels is beyond our capacity for calculation.

Cardinal Newman charmingly suggested that our own spirituality should make angels less mysterious to us than animals are. There is a wonderful pathos in Newman's remark, since animals are far better known to our scientists than they were in Newman's era, while angels seem more unknowable all the time. If we do not recognize our own spirituality, then how can we be attentive to angels? The great Thomistic insight is that angels have perfect knowledge of their own spirituality and so of their own freedom. We stumble about, knowing nothing but facts, while angels are great Platonists, as it were, and know the Ideas directly, yet also know all the facts. Our capacity to love is frequently founded upon romance, which is necessarily the realm of imperfect knowledge; angels, like God, love with perfect knowledge. Saint Thomas hardly intended this as an irony, but it cuts against us now by exposing all eros as being ironical. When Saint Thomas sets limits to angelic knowledge, they are temporal: God knows the future, but the angels may not, since their pathos is that they themselves may not be eternal. For me, the most surprising of Thomistic admonitions is that angels, unlike God, cannot know the inwardness of women and men, though the angels are superb at making surmises. One can ponder the limitations of all those guardian angels now cherished in America if they cannot know the hearts of those they seek to protect.

Saint John of the Cross, greatest of Spanish mystics, beautifully said that God only to himself is neither strange nor new; even the holiest of the angels are perpetually surprised by God. A French Catholic scholar, P. R. Régamey, juxtaposes to Saint John of the Cross's observation the grand phrase of Bossuet, famous for his eloquence, who said of Christ in relation to men and angels that the Savior is "more our own head than theirs." Saint Paul and Saint Peter, as I have already observed, emphasized that the victory of Christ was a defeat for the angels, a severe contention that is fundamental to Catholic doctrine concerning the angels. Régamey attempts to explain this away, and yet it seems to have been a crucial part of the struggle of Paul and Peter against the Jewish Christians led by James, who may have been Christian Gnostics. The sectaries of the Dead Sea Scrolls, once thought to be Essenes, seem now to have been a group who had more in common with the Jewish Christians and early Gnostics, and certainly saw themselves as being allied to angels, who would fight the final battles at their side. Islam, which developed from this Jewish Christianity, gave Christ the status of an angel, who could not be crucified, and so Islam rejected the Incarnation. Though modern Catholic exegetes tend to evade this split between Jewish and Pauline Christianity, there clearly is an opposition between the Incarnation and any exuberant angelology, an opposition that finds its classical statement in Saint Paul. It seems not too much to say that for Saint Paul every angel is potentially fallen until proven otherwise; the Apostle did not love, or trust, the angels. Like the Law of Moses, which Paul thought had been given by angels, the angels seemed to Paul to belong more to the Old Covenant than to the New.

Largely because of Saint Thomas, the Roman Catholic doctrine of angels is the most rational and orderly, though less imaginative than the visions of the Gnostics, Sufis, and Kabbalists. What Catholic doctrine shares with the traditions of Gnosis is an emphasis very much absent from our moment, which is the awesomeness or terrifying grandeur of the angels. This difference is one that I repeat, because our current domestication of the angels renders them insipid. It is not only the fallen spirits who are angels of destruction, and death itself after all is an angel. Yet the softening of angels was a long process, and a popular one, throughout the many Catholic centuries. By the sixteenth century, angels frequently were confounded with children, even with infants. This virtually ended the Aquinan notion that angels manifested "assumed bodies"; the form of an adult warrior or messenger could more readily be judged a fiction than a human baby. The popular imagination has achieved few triumphs more striking than the total transformation of the cherubim of Genesis, dread beings blocking the way back to Eden, into the baby cherubs of Western painting.

Saint Thomas rather movingly had a kind of Platonic nostalgia for the image of pure spirit, of intelligence unimpeded by the flesh and its urges. His angels occupy the gap between the human mind and the mind of God, and he reasoned that without the angels such a divide never could be bridged. Hierarchy required a chain of being, with differences in kind as well as degree distinguishing angels and humans. Since Aquinas subtly argued that God was (and is) free to create universes other than ours, and indeed more perfect than ours, the great theologian, for the honor of our cosmos, argued also that elements of pure spirit had been created by God for it. Angels, though awesome and terrible, are thus complements to us, and enhance our dignity.

Behind Aquinas was a general picture of reality all but universal in the medieval era, one neatly characterized by C. S. Lewis as "the Discarded Image," without which Catholic angelology would have lacked coherence. This image or model of reality begins with God in the Heaven of Heavens; power moves down from God through the spheres to the moon, and influence (or influx) radiates out from God's power, which in its unimpeded form is God's love for us. The separate spheres are regarded as Intelligences, a higher form of angels. The nine different ranks of angels, as accepted by Saint Thomas Aquinas, take us back to one of the three or four greatly misplaced writers in Western tradition, a fifth- or sixth-century C.E. Neoplatonist who wrote under the pseudonym of Dionysius the Areopagite. In the New Testament (Acts of the Apostles 17:34), Saint Paul speaks at Athens and is received badly by his Stoic and Epicurean auditors, some of whom mock his account of the resurrection of the dead. A few however are converted, including one named as Dionysius the Areopagite. In just what spirit we cannot know, Pseudo-Dionysius took on the identity of this honored convert, and his not very Christian writings acquired enormous prestige for many theologians, Thomas Aquinas among them. It was not until 1457, almost two centuries after the death of Aquinas, that the scholar Lorenzo Valla exposed the forgery, but by then the false Areopagite had shaped the Catholic hierarchy of the angels with rare permanence. This is certainly one of the major ironies of religious history, as there is very little that is Christian about Pseudo-Dionysius's heavenly structure, and everything that is Platonic or Neoplatonic. Thomas Aquinas is said by Jaroslav Pelikan to have quoted the Pseudo-Dionysius some 1,700 times, which simply would not have happened if only the great Scholastic had known that the author had written five centuries after Saint Paul had converted the as-it-were original Dionysius the Areopagite! The crucial work of the anonymous Neoplatonist is *The Celestial Hierarchy*, unquestionably the most important text in the entire history of angelology. "Hierarchy" appears to be a word invented by Pseudo-Dionysius, who follows the Neoplatonist Proclus by dividing everything into hierarchic triads. The hierarchies are the creation of Pseudo-Dionysius, but the categories of angels go back to Saint Ambrose, who took them from traditions whose origins are lost in time. There are three hierarchies, each of three orders, in descending ranks:

1. Seraphim
2. Cherubim
3. Thrones

4. Dominations
5. Virtues
6. Powers

7. Principalities
8. Archangels
9. Angels

Though Aquinas followed this ordering, Dante reversed the places of principalities and archangels. The seraphim traditionally surround God's throne, while endlessly chanting: "Holy, holy, holy." And yet there is only one reference to seraphim in the Hebrew Bible, the magnificent sixth chapter of the prophet Isaiah:

2 Above it stood the seraphims: each one had six wings;
with twain he covered his face, and with twain he covered his
feet, and with twain he did fly.

3 And one cried unto another, and said, Holy, holy, holy,
is the Lord of hosts: the whole earth *is* full of his glory.

4 And the posts of the door moved at the voice of him
that cried, and the house was filled with smoke.

5 Then said I, Woe is me! I am undone; because I am a
man of unclean lips, and I dwell in the midst of a people of
unclean lips: for mine eyes have seen the King, the Lord of
hosts.

6 Then flew one of the seraphims unto me, having a live
coal in his hand, which he had taken with the tongs from off
the altar.

There are no seraphim in the New Testament, but they are
prominent in 2 Enoch and 3 Enoch, and their leadership is
sometimes attributed to Metatron or Michael, and sometimes to
Lucifer, the unfallen Satan. Cherubim are important in the Hebrew Bible, from the guards set to block our reentry into Eden
on to the golden creatures flanking the Ark of the Covenant in
Exodus 25:18, and then the four beings of Ezekiel's vision
(10:4), and the olive wood angels of Solomon's Temple in
Kings 6:23. Revelation 4:8, founded upon Ezekiel's prophecy,
presents the cherubim as six-winged holy animals replete with
open eyes scattered throughout their bodies. Gabriel and
Raphael are among the most prominent cherubim, and sometimes Lucifer-Satan is assigned to them also. Thrones, who
complete the first celestial triad, do not occur in the Hebrew
Bible, but figure widely in rabbinical legend, though their func-

tion tends to be obscure, perhaps because a substantial number of them followed Satan in the Fall.

Dominations, beginning the second triad, have the honor of being the oldest or original angels, but they have never excited much interest. However, the Virtues, the next grade down, fascinate because their function is to work miracles in our world, and to serve as the guardian angels that Jesus mentions in Matthew 18:10. They have the honor of being the two angels who flank Jesus in the Ascension, perhaps because of the text in Matthew. Powers, who complete the second triad, generally are seen as guardians of order, a kind of heavenly police, and were particularly resented by Saint Paul, presumably because he associated them with the Law that Jesus had superseded.

The third triad commences with Principalities, defenders of religion and frequently associated with particular continents or countries. In Tony Kushner's *Angels in America,* the angel is the Continental Principality of America and the playwright wickedly says of her that she appeared to Joseph Smith, the Mormon prophet, who however got her name and identity wrong. The archangels, according to 1 Enoch, are seven, namely Uriel, Raguel, Michael, Seraqael, Gabriel, Haniel, and Raphael, who are presumably also the seven angels of Revelation 8:2. But this means archangels in the general sense of chief angels; the hierarchal category is just above the common angels, who are simply messengers that arrive bearing God's decrees. The final order, angels proper, are so far away from God that their closeness to us ironically reinforces the Neoplatonic coldness of the Dionysian system. Saint Paul, with his distaste for the angels, always affirmed that Jesus was the only mediator between God and men, which is pragmatically contradicted by a ninefold hierarchal structure of the angels.

THE FALLEN ANGELS

Though angels, of our sort, originated in Persia and Babylonia, any account of the fallen angels probably should begin with the Hellenistic, second-century C.E. author Apuleius, best known for his splendid romance, *The Golden Ass,* but more influential ultimately as the author of an essay, "On the God of Socrates." Socrates' "god" was his *daemon,* a spirit neither human nor angelic, who mediated between the gods and Socrates. Apuleius identifies the *daemons* as inhabitants of the air, with bodies of so transparent a kind that we cannot see them but only hear them, as Socrates did his *daemon.* Nevertheless, the daemons are material, as are the gods; it was the innovation of Thomas Aquinas to regard the angels, the equivalent of the gods, as pure spirits. According to Apuleius, every one of us has an individual guardian, and genius. By the later Middle Ages, these *daemons* also were identified with the fallen angels, or "demons," as they certainly were by Aquinas. C. S. Lewis ventured that Saint Paul ultimately was behind this, since in Ephesians 2:2 Paul wrote of "the prince of the power of the air, that now worketh in the children of disobedience," which was taken to refer to the *daemons* as Satanic beings.

Though it is always surprising to realize that the Hebrew Bible truly has no fallen angels, they are in fact not a Judaic idea

during the long period of the Bible's composition. The Satan of the Book of Job is "the adversary," or prosecuting attorney, a servant of God in good standing, and in no way evil. Again, in Isaiah 14:12–15, when the prophet sings the fall of *Helel ben Shahar,* the morning star, the reference indubitably is to the King of Babylon, and not to a fallen angel, as Christian interpreters have believed:

> 12 How art thou fallen from heaven, O Lucifer, son of the morning! how art thou cut down to the ground, which didst weaken the nations!
>
> 13 For thou hast said in thine heart, I will ascend into heaven, I will exalt my throne above the stars of God: I will sit also upon the mount of the congregation, in the sides of the north:
>
> 14 I will ascend above the heights of the clouds; I will be like the Most High.
>
> 15 Yet thou shalt be brought down to hell, to the sides of the pit.

Magnificent as this King James phrasing is, it radically distorts the Hebrew text, since "Lucifer" is simply the "Shining One," and "hell" is the rather different "Sheol," a kind of Hades. Similarly, Christian interpretation followed Aprocryphal literature in reading the *b'ne ha Elohim,* or sons of the Elohim, in Genesis 6:1–4 as being the sinful fallen angels, or "sons of God," who in the Enoch books marry earthly women in order to beget monstrous giants. The actual Yahwistic text of Genesis 6:1–4 has no moral tonality, and instead offers a perhaps ironic praise of "the mighty men that were of old, the men of renown" as being the issue of these unequal marriages. Something of the same pattern of misreading emerges in the Christian understanding of Psalm 82, a curiously mixed poem which seems to allegorize the wicked rulers of the nations as being the Elohim whom God condemns to die like mortal men. The same ambiguity enters into Ezekiel 28:12–19, a vision of the Prince of Tyre falling from the position of "the covering cherub," guarding Eden, and being cast "out of the mountain of God," again clearly a political prophecy, but interpeted by Christians as another reference to the fall of Lucifer into Satan. The largest and most famous Christian expansion is the metamorphosis of the subtle serpent of Eden into Satan, for which there is of course not the slightest basis in the Yahwist's text. About the only passages in the Hebrew Bible proper that refer to pragmatically bad or evil angels occur in Daniel 10:13–21 and 12:1, where Gabriel and Michael as guardian angels of Israel are set against their opposing angels of Persia and Greece. Even there we are not given an explicit prophecy that the guardian angels of the Gentile nations are condemned to fall, or perhaps already are "fallen angels."

The emergence of the Christian Satan and his fallen host was a complex process, but with very eclectic sources. Neil Forsyth's *The Old Enemy* traces the Devil to Huwawa, opponent of the Sumerian hero Gilgamesh, and to the equally rancid Humbaba, among the Assyrians. Many others got into the blend, including Tiamat, the Babylonian sea dragon, and Ahriman, the adversary according to Zoroaster. Yet one feels that there is a radically new element in the Christian Satan, because there is no room whatsoever for him in Yahwistic literature, even though Jewish apocalyptic texts later make a space for him, particularly in the Enoch books, the Wisdom of Solomon, and the Life of Adam. But there still is a leap from these to the New Testament, where Satan is truly an original invention, since he concentrates sin on a scale far more totally and powerfully than we might expect. The English Romantic poet Shelley liked to say that Satan owed everything to the English seventeenth-century Puritan poet Milton, but I suspect that Shelley would have agreed with me that the Devil's true debt was to Saint Augustine, the fourth-century C.E. Christian theologian, indeed to this day the greatest theologian in the two-thousand-year-old history of Christianity. Superb intellect as he was, Augustine bears the ultimate responsibility for molding the Christian Satan, who occupies a vital position in *The City of God,* the Augustinian masterwork. It is from *The City of God* that we learn the central story of Satan's rebellion, which is prompted by pride, and which *precedes the creation of Adam,* so that Satan's seduction of Adam and Eve comes after the fall of the angels. Elsewhere in Augustine we are confronted by his most original notion, the highly un-Hebraic doctrine that Adam and Eve and their descendants were created by God for the single purpose of replacing the fallen angels. This leads to the least Hebraic idea in Christianity: by their own fall, Adam and Eve and their progeny are eternally guilty and predisposed to sin, particularly in regard to obedience and to sexuality. Only the atoning sacrifice of the incarnate Christ, as defined by Saint Paul, Augustine's precursor, can free us from our guilt.

Satan and his subordinates were thus permanently stationed at the heart of the Christian story, which seems to me as radical a departure from Yahwistic religion as the Incarnation itself was. But since the fallen angels are my concern here, I need to return to the later Judaic and early Christian sources to worry the distinctions, such as they are, between unfallen angels and their sinful kin. Saint John the Divine, in chapter 12 of his Revelation, says that one angel in three fell, while Gustav Davidson, in his delightful *A Dictionary of Angels,* quotes a fifteenth-century bishop as setting the number of the fallen at a substantial 133,306,668. This figure would have appalled the early rabbis, since they followed the Hebrew Bible in attributing no evil impulses to the angels, for whom no divine law would have been too hard, doubtless another clue as to why Saint Paul so disliked angels. The problem surely is: how did wickedness come to inhabit so many of the angels in the Jewish Apocryphal literature? Norman Cohn culminates two hundred years of speculation by pointing to the influence of Zurvanite (revised Zoroastrian) doctrines of dualism upon the Jews of Maccabean times. I have no doubt but that Cohn is accurate: the names of the angels came from Babylon, and the evil nature of the fallen angels came from Persia. Zoroaster rather than the Yahwist or Isaiah is ironically the authentic ancestor of Saint Paul and Saint Augustine.

Since Saint Paul, in regard even to unfallen angels, was acutely ambivalent, I venture the hypothesis that the Incarnation of the Christ as Jesus made the angels somewhat superfluous, for they lost almost all function as mediators between man and God, once Christ had risen. Paul understood implicitly, long before Augustine, that the difference between Judaism and Christianity was between a belief that God's image survives in one even if partly hidden by sin, and a faith that the image was blotted out by sin except for the work of the Atonement. The angels, also being God's creatures and part of the cosmos, therefore are affirmed in their goodness by the Jews. But Paul has so keen a sense of the loss of God's image except in Christ, that for him even the greatest of the angels are equivocal beings, over whom Christ has triumphed.

To the extent that Christianity is essentially Pauline, it has no need and little use for virtuous angels. What Paul and Christianity needed were fallen angels, and their chief, Satan, in particular. We ought never to forget that, in the Hebrew Bible, "Satan" is not a proper name. In the Book of Job, the reader encounters *ha-Satan,* "the Satan," which is a court title, akin to our "prosecuting attorney." As one of the *b'ne Elohim,* the "sons of God," the Satan is a divine being, or angel, a *malak Yahweh,* or diplomatic representative of God. His title means something like "blocking agent": he is an authorized adversary of human beings. In Greek, a blocking agent is a *diabolos,* and so the Satan became diabolical. Forsyth in *The Old Enemy* traces the curious development of Satan among the Jews, by which a stumbling block became a scandal, and God's agent was transformed into an independent opponent of humankind, from a prosecutor to a persecutor, as it were. This metamorphosis was strange, considering how little it suited so strict a monotheism. The Apocryphal Enoch books became popular during the Hellenization of the Jews brought about by the conquests of Alexander the Great, and by the aftermath of the long wars fought between the rival generals who sought to inherit Alexander's empire. In the Little Genesis, or Book of Jubilees, probably written during the third century B.C.E., and influenced by the Enoch literature, the diabolic adversary is named Mastema, whose root is related to "Satan," and who has an ambiguous relation to the authority of God, since he is at once a rebel angel and yet still part of the cosmic scheme. A leap beyond this ambiguity is taken in the proto-Gnostic Adam books of the first century B.C.E., where Satan, identified as the serpent in Eden, is a rebel angel responsible for the fall of Adam and Eve, who begin with a status higher than the angels, and resented by the angels, fallen and unfallen alike.

A greater leap, in kind as well as degree, takes place in the New Testament, where the Satan of the Revelation of Saint John the Divine is the full-scale archetype of all rebel angels ever since. War in Heaven, not mentioned elsewhere in the New Testament, results in the fall of one-third of the stars, or heavenly hosts, swept down by a serpentine Satan who now enjoys autonomy from God. The story in Revelation is the first phase of the three-step downfall of the rebel angels, in which Saint Paul's vision dominates the second phase, and Saint Augustine's doctrines will provide the third, definitive stage of the development. Paul's distaste for all angels I have noted already; its most remarkable expression comes in 2 Corinthians 11:14, where the Apostle warns that "Satan himself is transformed into an angel of light." Every angel of light was under suspicion by Paul, who attributed all his rivals, Jewish Christian and Gnostic, to the heretical influence of Satan. This attribution, original with Paul, will never leave us, since it has become deeply embedded in every variety of Christianity. And since Paul interpreted the Law of the Jews and Jewish Christians as the law of sin and death, it was all too natural for him to identify his opponents with the Devil. Thus in Ephesians 6:11–12, Paul utters the most eloquent of all his denunciations of the angels, who seem to be both fallen and unfallen:

> Put on the whole armor of God, that ye may be able to stand against the wiles of the devil.
> For we wrestle not against flesh and blood, but against principalities, against powers, against the rulers of the darkness of this world, against spiritual wickedness in high places.

Paul's influence upon the Church fathers was to eventuate in the image of Satan as Christ's envious younger brother, who seeks to usurp the Kingdom of God from Christ. Augustine culminates this tradition by carrying the division between Christ and Satan all the way back to the first day of Creation, when God divided the light from the darkness, and part of the angels chose the darkness, in an initial sin of pride. More subtle than Paul, Augustine had the originality to invent Satanic psychology, centering it upon envy and pride, thus creating the tradition that would ensue in the Iago of Shakespeare's *Othello* and the Satan of Milton's *Paradise Lost*. Yet Augustinian Satanic pride interests me less than the Pauline ambivalence towards all the angels, if only because angelic ambiguity has vanished all but completely from our current national obsession with angels. Even devout Christians seem to have repressed Paul's incessant distrust of the angels, which nevertheless is at the heart of his polemic against Christian Judaizers and Christian Gnostics. He feared worship of the angels, and of the Law given by the angels, even as he ironically shared in the Gnostic traditions of distrust and rivalry between Adam and the angels. Perhaps Paul chose to misunderstand the angels even as he chose to misunderstand the Law; observance of Torah was never justification (as he said) but only an obedience to Yahweh's will, and the angels were never justified except as an expression of that will.

The return of angelicism to America is not a new event; it reflects rather a tradition that has prevailed since the nineteenth century, when it culminated in the most American of religions, Mormonism. Paul and Augustine would have frowned upon our angelic obsessions, and both the Catholics and normative Protestants ought to be most uneasy with this current in our popular spirituality. And yet it is very American, and represents another return of an ancient gnosis that official Christianity fought to annihilate.

ANGELS, MIRACLES, AND AMERICA

How is it that Ezekiel and Daniel, and the Gnostic, Sufi, and Kabbalist sages, and Saint Francis and Saint Teresa and Joseph Smith, could see angels, and we cannot? Contemporary accounts of angelic sights are unpersuasive, whether the personage sighted be a traditional angel, or an alien transported via UFO. Wiser heads among our current angelologists are resigned to sensing the presence of angels, rather than seeing and hearing them. I do not doubt that the long succession of seers from Zoroaster through Joseph Smith actually saw and heard appropriate angels, even as I am greatly skeptical of our ongoing fashions in angelic encounters. There has been an authentic change from the Enlightenment onwards, with only a few throwbacks like Swedenborg, William Blake, and Joseph Smith. Human nature changes, and miracles and angels ebb away. How and why?

The phenomenon is one of distancing, temporal rather than spatial. What has been distanced is neither empirical nor spiritual, but all the connections in between, and time is the agent of that estrangement. Angels violate the law of nature, a law however not in effect until the later seventeenth century. Perhaps the law of nature was discovered then; perhaps it was imposed, as William Blake insisted. Either way, angels are not random facts, but no seer to whom they came ever considered them as such anyway.

Messengers are useless if they have no message to deliver, and no one to send them. Reading endless accounts of alien visitations, one wonders why the people who assert that they have been abducted or invaded invariably are not particularly gifted or very intelligent. The same melancholy wonder is provoked by the more benign and traditional angel guardians of recent accounts. Angels have mattered only because the humans who confronted them have mattered greatly. Gabriel sought out the prophet Muhammad, who had the creative imagination of a Dante or a Milton. Moroni chose Joseph Smith, an extraordinary religious genius. If authentic angelic descents accompany the approach of the second Millennium, they will be made to true prophets, who have not yet appeared among us. This is both the effective comic pathos and the ultimate aesthetic weakness of Tony Kushner's *Angels in America,* where his gallant, ill gay prophet simply has no prophecy to give us.

Angels, from our perspective, have to be human rather than divine events. God does not need to believe in angels; if we do, we have to make sense of that belief, so that the law of nature is violated to some purpose. Otherwise, angels would be only blasphemies, insults to the Creation. The Koran teaches this crucial lesson more overtly than the Bible does, and such teaching revives Judaic and Christian truths, as Muhammad insisted. An angel cannot intervene, or be invoked, by whim, his or ours: it must be by a greater will, not to be usurped by believer or by skeptic. At our late moment, in the shadow of the Millennium, necessary angels will be very subtle angels, because gross miracles no longer suit us. The Dutch psychiatrist J. H. Van den Berg, in his shrewd introduction to a "historical psychology," *The Changing Nature of Man,* is my mentor here:

> But whether the miracle is a fact *contra naturam* depends ultimately on our conception of nature. If nature is understood to be the reality of science—in other words, a reality distilled from the other, total, general, daily reality by a narrowly circumscribed, uncommon, acquired, and in every way artificial, point of view—then, indeed, miracles involve things so far removed from their common nature that they can no longer show the presence of God. . . . God has been removed from reality so thoroughly that it is impossible for Him to appear. If within this conception of nature God is still expected to appear, it will have to be assumed that He can appear as a physical fact among other physical facts, as a

child for instance: as the child Jesus, who plays between the oak tree and the maple tree, and who can be approached in the same biological way as the trees can be approached. Believing in the miracle in this way is actually not believing in it. For in the first place, reality—which is, above all, a realization of our understanding with God—has been reduced to a system of scientific facts; this means that God has been removed from this reality. And in the second place, if He is then, after all, requested to reappear in this reality, which has become foreign to Him, in the shape of an "objective" fact among other "objective" facts, then, this means that God dies. The conception that the miracle is *contra naturam* does not only mean that, as a miracle, it disrupts nature; it also implies that the miracle which appears in the resulting cleft shows itself as a (pseudo) natural, (pseudo) physical, and (pseudo) chemical fact. Belief in the miracle . . . is belief in (pseudo) science.

Substitute "angel" for "miracle" throughout this paragraph, and you arrive at an unanswerable insight that accounts for why we had better credit any angelic sightings now and hereafter only when they are reported by prophets, seers, and revelators, or by great poets. Belief in angels, by most of us, is belief in false miracles, and is an offense against God, unless you really do espouse a magical, or spiritual, or metaphoric view of nature. Joseph Smith lived in an America where a magical worldview was still common among the folk, as Vincent Quinn has shown. Doubtless, another American religious genius will appear, though we will not know her (at first) when she does. For now, I would urge everyone concerned with angels, prophetic dreams, "near-death experiences," and the oncoming Millennium to measure our current encounters with these phenomena against the best that has been known and written about them in the past. That is the primary purpose of this book: to raise up and illuminate these appearances in order to save them, by returning them to the interpretive wisdom of the Christian Gnostics, Muslim Sufis, and Jewish Kabbalists. Without a context that can serve as a spiritual standard of measurement, we will drown in New Age enthusiasms and wish fulfillments.

The Catholic Church, true to its traditions, insists always that angels are closer to God than to man, and tends also to emphasize the otherness of the angels. In Protestant and post-Protestant America, this otherness has waned, and threatens now to vanish altogether. In the vivid epiphany of Gabriel to Daniel, the prophet first loses consciousness in shock and terror, and recovers himself only when touched benignly by the angel. I juxtapose to Daniel's spiritual trauma the treacle of our popular angel manuals, one of which actually suggests that there are cat angels, who presumably manifest themselves to our cats. The domestication of angels makes them dull and saccharine, and reminds me of the actress Jane Russell's theological outburst on television, when at a late moment in her career she took up singing spirituals, and defined God thusly: "I think that God is just a livin' doll!"

Whether we interpret them as God's messengers, or his warriors, or even his administrators, angels are meaningless apart from God, even when they are in rebellion against him. Palpable as this is, we are wise to keep reminding ourselves of it. To an atheist or skeptic, angels can have no reality, and yet the best of modern American poets, the unbelieving Wallace Stevens, invokes what he calls "the angel of reality" in his work. Avicenna, the great Persian physician, mystic, and philosopher of the eleventh century, transfigured Koranic angelology into a highly imaginative doctrine that has curious affinities with twentieth-century secular poets who celebrate angels, Stevens and the German visionary, R. M. Rilke, in particular. In Avicenna's angelology, the monotheistic cosmos of the Koran tends to be dispersed into a kind of pragmatic polytheism, much resented by literalist orthodoxy in Islam, both now and then. The tension in all angelology, then and now, is between monotheism and the elevation of other heavenly beings to a status that seems to rival God's. And yet the major monotheisms—Zoroastrianism, Judaism, Christianity, Islam—are all pervaded by angels.

It is an ancient pattern among monotheists that the gods of other faiths and nations are demoted to the status of angels (or of demons). As guardian angels of rival states, these former gods easily could be associated with evil and with pestilence. The solitary eminence of Yahweh prevented the Jews from developing a full-scale, overt mythology, though there are many traces of such polytheistic inventiveness before the resurgence of the "Yahweh alone" spirit that seems to commence with the prophet Hosea in the eighth century B.C.E. When that spirit triumphs in Deuteronomy, the way was prepared for a religion of Yahweh almost purged of any angelology. It was not until the Maccabees rose against the Hellenized Syrians that angelology returned fiercely in the Book of Daniel and later in the non-

canonical works; yet the revival of Judaic angelology was begun long before, during the Babylonian exile. Here the prophet
Ezekiel is the decisive figure; his vision of the Chariot, "the
Wheels and their Work," is the true starting point for all subsequent Judaic angelology and esotericism, and must qualify as
supreme among all angel epiphanies.

There is, as we will see, an ancient tradition of enmity between the fallen angels and Adam, and an even more archaic rivalry between good angels and the first man. Saint Paul may be
the figure in whom all of the tensions between angels and humans came together. Like Augustine after him, Paul is so central
to Christianity, both Catholic and Protestant, that the current
prevalence of angel worship among us is an even more extraordinary phenomenon than initially it may seem to be. We forget the Pauline admonitions because, slowly but massively,
an American angelology is developing among us, and not just
among the Mormons, and the Pentecostals, and New Age networks, but among Roman Catholics, Southern Baptists, Jews,
and across the religious spectrum. We always have been a religiously fecund nation, particularly from about 1800 on. Since
our religion tends to be experiential and pragmatic, it increasingly has departed from European Christianity, where the institutional, historical, and theological aspects of the faith have
remained relatively strong. Since we tend to be heterodox, even
when we assert otherwise, angels return to us from the spiritual
repression that Saint Paul inaugurated. For us, they become images of our freedom: from the past, from authority, from the necessity of dying. And for many among us, I suspect, the angels

are well-nigh independent of God. Like the American Jesus, who is primarily the Jesus of the Resurrection, rather than of the Crucifixion or the Ascension, our angels are versions of the Jewish Christian, Gnostic, and Muslim Angel Christ. Each guardian angel intimates the possibility of a personal resurrection, if not at the onset of the coming Millennium, then perhaps at a third of a century beyond it.

In chapter 4 of this book, on Gnosis, I will elaborate a similar pattern among the Sufis and Kabbalists. Since there are no direct links between contemporary angelic obsessions and earlier esotericists, some explanation needs to be sought for these parallels. If one is a Jungian, which I am not, there would be nothing to explain: we would be dealing with archetypes of the collective unconscious. The likelier interpretation is that ancient, medieval, and modern Gnosis all seek to answer an authentic and lasting spiritual need, which is to reconcile time and death with our intimations of immortality.

There is an anonymous midrash in which Jacob says to Moses: "I am greater than you; I encountered an angel and conquered him," to which Moses replies: "You encountered the angel in your domain, but I ascended to the Ministering Angels in their domain, and they were afraid of me. . . ." Let us assume that Jacob overcame Sammael, Angel of Death, the guardian angel of his wronged brother Esau, and let us surmise also that Moses, not dying but translated to Heaven by the kiss of Yahweh, affronted the angels even as the unfallen Adam and Enoch-Metatron frightened them. Like Enoch and Elijah (who became Sandalphon), Moses ascended in order to perform service for

Yahweh, but there is no name for the angelic Moses. I always have wondered why; the rabbis sometimes called Moses an angel, yet some texts accord Moses a rank above all the angels, even Metatron. That may be the answer; even as the New Testament reminds the angels that their status is below Jesus', so the Hebrew Bible implicitly honors Moses above the angels. There is an esoteric tradition that Jesus was an angel, one of the two who appeared with Yahweh under the terebinths at Mamre, there to accept Abraham's hospitality. Jacob, who became Israel, is sometimes identified as or with the angel Uriel (with whom Emerson had the audacity to seek identification). There is a Franciscan tradition, highly heterodox and esoteric, that Saint Francis alone shared the distinction of Enoch, Elijah, and Jacob, as a fourth mortal transformed into an angel. Rhamiel, the angel of mercy, is the final form of Saint Francis, holding off the winds of destruction until all of the redeemed are gathered up into Heaven.

There is clearly a tension between this image of four patriarchs and prophets—Enoch, Jacob, Elijah, Saint Francis—translated to angelic status, and the warnings of the rabbis and of Saint Paul against a religion of the angels, warnings peculiarly appropriate in the present age. And yet millennial America always has welcomed angels, a welcome particularly manifested in the traditions of the Church of Jesus Christ of Latter-Day Saints, Joseph Smith's Mormons. Smith, the inaugural Mormon prophet, seer, and revelator, received three nocturnal visits from Moroni, a previously unknown angel, on September 21, 1823, in Palmyra, New York. The angel's message concerned a book "written upon gold plates, giving an account of the former inhabitants of this continent, and the sources from when they sprang." Yet four years intervened before Moroni found Smith worthy of the mission of translating the new sacred book, which did not appear until early in 1830. Since the Book of Mormon itself is a work of angelic authorship, Mormonism necessarily is profoundly involved in angelology. Whether one takes the vision of the angels as divine revelation received by Smith, or as the product of his indubitable religious genius, the Mormon doctrine of angels is of extraordinary interest, both for its own intrinsic power and for its illumination of the American longing for angelic realities. My principal sources here are a useful volume, *Angels*, by Oscar W. McConkie, Jr. (1975), and the researches of D. B. Timmins, a Mormon scholar-diplomat. Timmins remarks that Joseph Smith divided angels into three classes:

1. Pre-mortal spirits sent to earth with messages for authentic believers; these spirits later will undergo human birth.
2. "Just men made perfect": the righteous who have lived and died on earth, and who are sent to perform missions that pre-mortal spirits would not have had the experience to understand. These righteous are divided into two subgroups: those not yet resurrected, and those with a consubstantial post-resurrection body of flesh and bones (but no blood, which is merely mortal).

3. Lucifer and his deceivers, who (as in Paul) masquerade as "angels of light."

Moroni evidently was of the second subgroup in class 2, a resurrected being. All four kinds of angels look alike; Moroni's appearance to Joseph Smith reminds me of Gabriel's in the Book of Daniel, and is parallel to Gabriel's appearance to the prophet Muhammad. Even as Muhammad is "the seal of the prophets," the final messenger, for Islam, so Smith is for his Latter-Day Saints. While Muhammad remains just that for Islam, Mormonism is a more radical doctrine, and Joseph Smith doubtless by now is a resurrected angel, another god-man, working for the welfare of the world's 10 million or so Mormons. One sees why Smith was fascinated by Enoch, and actually identified himself with that extraordinary being. In his own final phase, Smith evidently studied Kabbalah, and came to understand that as the resurrected Enoch his ultimate transformation would be into the angel Metatron, the "lesser Yahweh," who is also the angel Michael and resurrected Adam. Though orthodox Islam refuses such an identification for Muhammad, the Sufis insisted upon it, and Joseph Smith thus brings together (whether he knew it or not) the three great esoteric traditions of Christian Gnosticism, Sufism, and Kabbalah.

Oscar McConkie details a few of the vast Mormon memorials of angelic visitations; perhaps because these are molded by tradition, they seem to me the exception that troubles my deep skepticism of contemporary American accounts of angelic manifestations. Joseph Smith had set forth the very American and pragmatic principle that angels can and should perform only what we cannot accomplish for ourselves. As always, I am moved by the prophet Joseph's wisdom, which would go a long way to correct the excesses and self-indulgences of our media-driven and commercialized exploitation of angelic imagery. The operative principle at our moment seems to be the exact inverse of Joseph Smith's admonition: hosts of deluded souls now implore angels to do for us what we should do for ourselves.

CHAPTER 2

REAMS

THE ANSWERING ANGEL

In the little town of Safed, in northern Palestine, Kabbalah flourished throughout the sixteenth century. The great figures were Moses Cordovero, a fecund systematizer of Kabbalah, and his student Isaac Luria, unquestionably the most original speculator ever to appear among Kabbalists. Luria belonged to the oral tradition; he wrote little, and what is most vital in him did not get into his writing and survived only because his disciples preserved his conceptions in their works. After Cordovero and Luria, the most renowned mystic of the Safed circle was Joseph Karo, whose major effort went into what is still the codification of Jewish Law, the *Shulhan Arukh*. Karo's mystical side centered upon his long relationship with the angelic voice, or *maggid*, who functioned as an alternative self. There is an eminent study of Karo by R. J. Zwi Werblowsky (1962), which concentrates upon the *maggid*, Karo's "Answering Angel," who dictated a mystical diary to the learned Karo. This diary, written in the Aramaic of the *Zohar*, the masterwork of Kabbalah, is preserved only in fragments, and is a startling document, one that confounds all preconceived notions about the nature of normative Judaism. Karo after all is nearly as definitive of Judaism as Maimonides; both set the pattern of observance of the Law. Yet Karo's *maggid* is almost the wildest of all Kabbalistic phenomena, being a *man-made angel*, though by no means unique in the spiritual world of sixteenth-century Safed.

That the *maggid*, or "Answering Angel," should be a human creation seems to me the hidden key to the later Kabbalah of Isaac Luria. Kabbalah, like earlier Jewish speculation, knows of angels created by God's word just to perform a brief specific function, of use or praise, after which they cease to be. Nowhere could Jewish tradition (so far as I know) have conceived of what Luria's disciple, Hayim Vital, called angels born of Torah or of holy acts:

> And now let us explain the subject of prophecy and the Holy Spirit.... It is *impossible* that anything that comes out of man's mouth should be in vain and there is nothing that is completely ineffective ... for every word that is uttered creates an angel.... Consequently, when a man leads a righteous and pious life, studies the Law, and prays with devotion, then angels and holy spirits are created from the

sounds which he utters . . . and these angels are the mystery of *maggidim,* and everything [i.e., the quality and dignity of these *maggidim*] depends on the measure of one's good works.

There are *maggidim* which deceive a little, for though they are holy and their root is in the side of holiness, yet [the imperfection of] the human act [that brought them into existence] caused them [to be imperfect].

Everything depends on the quality of the human act. Sometimes the *maggidim* are true and sometimes there are such as tell lies. Therefore it is said of Samuel [1 Samuel 3:19 "and the Lord was with him and did let none of his words fall to the ground"]; this is the case when he [the *maggid*] can substantiate his words. . . . Another criterion is that all his words be for the sake of heaven [i.e., conducive to perfection] . . . another criterion is that he expound kabbalistic doctrines and mysteries. But the reason that an angel can tell lies is this: since his creation results from the actions of man, therefore his nature will be in accordance with these actions. If someone studies the Law with pure intent and without ulterior motives, then, corresponding, the angel created thereby will be exceedingly holy and exalted and true in all his words; similarly if one reads the Law without making mistakes.

Werblowsky acutely characterizes Vital's speculations as being based "on a really terrifying conviction of the potency and significance of every human act." These belated angels of Safed Kabbalah are fascinatingly unstable, in ways appropriate to the dream realms that they govern. Answering Angels give dream answers to waking questions, but they break into the waking dimension entirely when they speak through the mouth of the prophet, independently of his will. A diagnosis of demoniac possession or schizoid manifestation seems to me absurd when applied to the saintly mystics of Safed, and is scarcely as persuasive as their own speculation of possession by a *maggid,* or Answering Angel. The great rabbis of Safed, persons of learning and genius, intellectually questioned each *maggid* so as to establish angelic reliability and veracity. Rather charmingly, the Answering Angel had to pass a strict examination in order to establish credentials in Kabbalistic erudition, the quest for holiness, and goodwill towards all "for the sake of heaven." Yet despite all safeguards, the Answering Angel remains the most shocking innovation in the entire history of angelology. We are moving towards phenomena different only in degree, not in kind, that will culminate in the creation of the Golem attributed to the Kabbalistic rabbi of Prague, Judah Loew ben Bezalel, who is supposed to have long preceded Mary Shelley's Dr. Victor Frankenstein in making a daemon or monster. The principle involved surely is the same, and we wonder at the audacity of the great Kabbalists of Safed, who certainly risked the sin of displacing God as the creator. Perhaps that risk accounts both for the Safed rabbis' original association of the Answering Angels with the realm of the angel Metatron, and their mysterious substitution of the prophet Elijah for Enoch as the human transformed into "the lesser Yahweh," Metatron.

Since the Torah's words were those of God, the shock that angels are born of its words might be somewhat lessened, except that the Kabbalists read not only the words but the letters, *and* the spaces in between the letters and the words, and interpretations of these gaps also brought forth angels. Acts of interpretation and good deeds hardly were distinguished by the Safed mystics, certainly an alarming tendency when professional interpreters stop to consider the consequences of their labors. Angels upon angels, angels everywhere, thronged the atmosphere of Safed in the sixteenth century, and the most remarkable among them, like the *maggid* of Joseph Karo, made "mighty promises" as dream interpreters prophesying the personal future, including the martyrdom that Karo strangely desired: to be burned for the sanctification of God's name. Fortunately the *maggid* was wrong, and Karo died of natural causes at the substantial age of eighty-seven. The Talmud says that a dream is only one-sixtieth part of prophecy, so presumably even the holiest of Answering Angels who govern the dream realm can mistake the future. Normative Judaism, in any case, always insisted that there can be no authority assigned to preternatural phenomena, and the Kabbalists of Safed were all Talmudists of repute, Karo above all others. It becomes therefore a very nice point as to how much trust or credence Karo could place in his *maggid* without himself being rendered uneasy.

Werblowsky implies that this was not a problem for Karo; doubtless there is so vast a difference between any spirituality available to most of us, and Safed in its great era, that we have great difficulty in fully recovering Karo's perspective. The quasi-automatic speech of a *maggid* is not altogether different from current Pentecostalism, but that is not a Jewish phenomenon, and Karo's *maggid* is fiercely intellectual, in contrast to Pentecostalists who speak with the tongues of men and of an-

maggid are the created angels

gels. The paradox of a rational (rather than rationalized) mode of possession by the Answering Angel remains to be investigated.

Less radical than Vital, who presumably adhered strictly to Luria's teachings, the great systematizer Cordovero (certainly the best intellect to appear among Kabbalists) never allowed himself to write that angels were a human creation. Yet even Cordovero says that "the mystery of Metatron" governs Answering Angels, meaning that the more someone resembles the prophet Elijah in word and in deed, the more likely that an angel will speak through one, giving dream answers to wakeful queries. This is still the intervention of a *maggid,* and therefore a singular manifestation, however attested as to its holiness. One feels that the more imaginative Luria was psychologically shrewder than his teacher Cordovero in assigning a state of possession to a spirit of man's own creation. Responsibility therefore devolves upon the individual, and so in some sense the narrator of the dream and its interpreter ultimately are one.

This returns us to the sources of all Judaic dream interpretation, to Joseph in Genesis. Joseph begins his career as interpreter by the dangerous procedure of recounting his dreams to his brothers and then expounding the meanings for his jealous rivals. Freud would not acknowledge Joseph as his precursor, but the parallels are clear enough: in both masters of dream self-interpretation, the driving force and the meaning of the dream work come together under the guise of the dreamer's own ambition. Both Joseph and Freud are what Freud charmingly called conquistadors. Ironically the atheist Freud seems as divinely favored as the charismatic Joseph, of whom the Tyndale translation of the Bible charmingly says: "Now Joseph was a lucky fellow, and God was with him." Joseph, unlike the Safed Kabbalists, required no Answering Angel. Joseph's brothers sensibly hated him all the more "for his dreams and his words," because they recognized the shrewd authority in his prophetic interpretations, which accurately predicted his eventual rule over them. I will resume an account of Joseph in the final section of this chapter, "Prophecy and Dreams," since here I need to return to the ambivalent figure of the Answering Angel.

An angel-interpreter of the dream whose capacity for deceit depends upon the relative virtue of his human creator is a remarkable image for the equivocal nature of dreams, and for the dangers of foretelling through the medium of dreams. As Talmudic scholars, the Kabbalists of Safed necessarily founded their ideas of dream interpretation upon the Babylonian Talmud, and on the tractate *Berakhot* especially, since it gathers together an immense mass of material on the meaning of dreams. Ken Frieden, in his lucid *Freud's Dream of Interpretation* (1990), notes that many of the rabbis cited in *Berakhot* disagree with one another on the origins of dreams, some insisting that dreams are granted by angels, while others ascribe them to evil spirits. Against both these theories, which alike regard dreams as flawed, minor prophecies, are the judgments of other ancient rabbis: that any person's dream is displayed to him only from "the thoughts of his own heart." Few statements about dream prophecy are more poignant than the skepticism of Rabbi Chrisda: "The sadness of a bad dream is sufficient to it, and the joy of a good dream is sufficient to it." Frieden aptly comments: "The impression arises that the response to a dream is even more decisive than the dream itself; *Berakhot* gradually refutes the assumption that dreams are intrinsically good or bad."

But how then can dreams be prophetic, since true prophecy, the Talmud affirms, is always from God? The ancient rabbis understood, at least as well as we do, that dreams are wanting both in literal truth and also in power of unrestricted imagination. We are neither prophets nor poets when we dream, but only such stuff that must submit to interpretation. The dream itself *can* be a kind of minor prophecy, but even then it is subject to a wise rabbinical adage: "There is no dream without worthless things." Even wiser is a story told by *Berakhot*, in which Rabbi Bana'ah takes his one dream to two dozen separate interpreters: "Each interpreted differently, and all of their interpretations were fulfilled. . . . All dreams follow the mouth." What would Sigmund Freud have replied to a suggestion that his *Interpretation of Dreams* should take as its epigraph that wonderful Talmudic irony: "All dreams follow the mouth"? Long since, I have written that sentence onto the title page of every edition I possess of Freud's extraordinary dream book, at once his masterpiece yet also an outrageous imposition of his genius upon material that would not yield even to his Faustian will. Freud, as I will show later in this chapter, was his own Answering Angel, and his self-fulfilling, prophetic interpretations fade away as we approach Millennium, when more than ever all dreams will follow the mouth.

The Nature of Dreams

Aristotle, in his brief treatise *On Prophesying by Dreams,* declines either to reject or accept such divination or prophetic dreaming, yet observes that "it is absurd to combine the idea that the sender of such dreams should be god with the fact that those to whom he sends them are not the best and wisest, but merely commonplace persons." The dreamer's status or quality is an unstable factor in all dream narration and dream interpretation, from the ancients until now. More than one dream anthology has cited the pre-Socratic sage Heraclitus, who emphasized the idiosyncratic element in the dreamer's realm: "When we are awake, we have one common world; but when we are asleep each turns aside to a world of his own." This is akin to his insistence that while the true way is one, nevertheless the mass of mankind maintain each their own private opinion, so Heraclitus clearly places no credence in dreams. Artemidorus, author of the earliest *Interpretation of Dreams* (about 150 C.E.), begins the other tradition, of honoring the dream, which can be said to culminate in Jung, even as Freud returns to Heraclitus. Freud treats the dream as his opponent whom he must wrestle and subdue. In status, a dream and a hallucination are all but identical for Freud, so that (rather oddly) Freud is compelled pragmatically to regard the dream as an illness that he must cure. I cannot think of a larger departure from worldwide dream traditions than this Freudian attitude, but I will defer considering it until the next section of this chapter.

The Talmudic Rabbi Hisda had said that "An uninterpreted dream is like an unread letter." That is already Freudian enough, and is at an opposite pole from the Neoplatonist view, which insisted that dreams came from the higher spheres, and had transcendental value. Whether this was a difference that made a difference is unclear to me, since the Neoplatonists also insisted that we must all submit ourselves to the interpretation of dreams. It is fascinating that so much of the theological tradition—Judaic and Catholic—tends to agree with Freud's devaluation of the dream. Maimonides quoted the Sages as teaching that "Dream is the unripe fruit of prophecy," and Saint Thomas Aquinas is highly ambivalent about divination by dreams. In contrast, the Protestant John Calvin warned us not to neglect the dreams that we tended not to remember, since they *might* be from God. There is a skeptical undercurrent towards everything connected with dreams, even in Calvin, which dominates the Protestant tradition. The most eloquent expression of this is by the seventeenth-century physician and speculator, skeptic and believer, Sir Thomas Browne:

If some have swounded [fainted] they may have also dyed in dreames, since death is butt a confirmed swounding. Whether Plato dyed in a dreame, as some deliver, hee must rise agayne to informe us. That some have never dreamed is as improbable, as that some have never laughed. That children dreame not the first half yeare, that men dreame not in some Countries, with many more, are unto mee sick mens dreames, dreames outt of the Ivorie gate, and visions before midnight.

This wonderful blend of credulity and interpretive suspicion reappears many times in the philosophic tradition, and culminates in Nietzsche's charming employment of the dream to undermine what we normally call waking consciousness. With his customary aphoristic shrewdness, Nietzsche informed us that *dreams themselves are a mode of interpretation,* and that ordinary consciousness is no more, no less:

> Real life has not the freedom of interpretation possessed by dream life; it is less poetic and less unrestrained—but is it necessary for me to show that our instincts, when we are awake, likewise merely interpret our nervous irritations and determine their "causes" in accordance with their requirements, that there is no really essential difference between waking and dreaming? that even in comparing different degrees of culture, the freedom of the conscious interpretation of the one is not in any way inferior to the freedom in dreams of the other! that our moral judgments and valuations are only images and fantasies concerning physiological processes unknown to us, and a kind of habitual language to describe certain nervous irritations? that all our so-called consciousness is a more or less fantastic commentary on an unknown text, one which is perhaps unknowable but yet felt?
>
> —*The Dawn of Day*

There is a sense in which Freud, as an interpreter of dreams, prudently withdrew from this subversive Nietzschean perspectivism, which has more in common with Shakespeare, particularly with Hamlet, than with anyone else. Heroes of consciousness, Hamlet and Nietzsche alike question its authority. Freud also knew how treacherous consciousness was, partly because Freud knew Hamlet and Nietzsche, but in Freud such knowledge is ultimately deployed to strengthen consciousness against the world of the instincts or drives. To say of consciousness that it is a fantastic commentary on an unknown text necessarily denies all authority to one's own perspective; there is no secure place for one to stand. Freud refused that Hamlet-like abyss, because his project ostensibly was therapeutic as well as supposedly enlightening, but also because his dream book was a concealed spiritual autobiography, at whose center was his own, astonishing intellectual ambition. Yet that is the subject of this chapter's next section; more relevant to the nature of dreams would be the realization that Freud knew little and cared less about sleep. He believed that the only function of the dream was to keep us from waking, and he knew little about the different levels of sleep and their relation to dreaming.

Sleep essentially is a slackening of the muscles and of the mind, and it is worth recalling that several ancient traditions make sleep the brother of death. The pre-Socratic speculator, Empedocles, explains sleep as a cooling of the blood caused by the separation of fire away from the three other elements. Modern sleep research truly began with Nathaniel Kleitman and Hans Berger, who between them established the two most remarkable truths concerning sleep. Berger, during the 1920s, discovered that sleep is accompanied by the rise of electrical brain waves (called electroencephalograms, or EEGs for short). Kleitman in 1952 came upon the phenomenon of rapid eye movement (REM) sleep, during which our dreaming takes place. REM sleep is fundamentally different from all of the four stages of non-REM sleep, during which sleep becomes progressively deeper. There tend to be two periods of REM sleep per night, averaging between one and two hours together in length. Most dreams, according to reliable researchers, are quite dull and forgettable; the adage that, asleep, we are all geniuses or poets is untrue. Memorable dreams tend to be anxious or unhappy ones, though less so among children, even though they dream for longer periods. Alexander Borbely, in his *Secrets of Sleep* (1986), surprisingly tells us that the time span represented in a dream, and the actual time spent dreaming, frequently coincide, which would have startled Freud. He might also have been disturbed to learn that there is no real distinction between "dreamless sleep" and "dream sleep." REM sleep produces more vivid and intense dreams, and certainly more prolonged, but all sleep is marked by dreams.

It would also be difficult to reconcile Freud to the most interesting theories of dreams now current, first that of the Swiss researchers Lehmann and Koukkou, which holds that as we sleep we are at work revising our childhood conceptions with later formulations. Dreams therefore become the product of a revisionary process without which we could not survive. More drastic is the neurological theory of Francis Crick; Crick suggests that dreams are an unlearning process by which the brain gets rid of material it has found irrelevant during the previous day. Where Freud urges the patient to remember the dream, Crick urges us to forget, thus cooperating with the brain. Borbely points out that neither Lehmann-Koukkou nor Crick is verifiable, but neither can they be refuted, whereas much of Freud's repressed wish fulfillment is already a period piece.

In Homer the dream is a person or a god, frequently seeking to ward off impending disaster from a hero. That cultural identification is irrecoverable, though we remain haunted by the admonitory aura of certain dreams. As messengers, as guardians, as thresholds to transcendence, some of our dreams appear indistinguishable from angels, and may as well be seen as such. So they are regarded in the Sufism of Ibn 'Arabi (1165–1240), as will be expounded in chapter 4, "Gnosis," but no general exposition of the nature of dreams should set aside the strongest of universal traditions, East and West, which associates angels and dreams. The Zoroastrian Avesta, the Bible, the Koran, and the Gnostics, Sufis, and Kabbalists all concur with Indian and Chinese sacred texts in treating dreams as divine epiphanies. Freud, who fought this at the overt level, yielded to it in his preoccupations with parapsychology, and we still have not resolved the mysteries of the dream. Our dream interpretation, whether among the Freudians or the neurological sleep researchers, is always reductive, seeking to interpret the dream downwards as it were. Yet our dreams manifestly do traffic in our fears and hopes for our futures; we freely associate most vigorously in our dreams, and unless we are rock-hard metaphysical materialists, we are bound to encounter intimations of transcendence in our dream worlds. Freud's mode was speculation, and so was Ibn 'Arabi's; to choose one over the other as an interpreter of dreams is not to choose irrationalism over rationalism, but rather one kind of speculation over another. I choose Ibn 'Arabi in this book, even though I am no more a mystic nor a normative believer than Freud ever was. Without falling into the arcana of the New Agers, one still searches for an imaginatively coherent and humanly adequate account of the nature of dreams, and Freud does not provide it. Shakespeare of course does, but so richly that we struggle to keep up with his complexities. Cleopatra tells Dolabella that she has dreamed of the dead Antony, yet concludes ambivalently as to the status of her dreams as against nature:

> But if there be, or ever were one such,
> It's past the size of dreaming: nature wants stuff
> To vie strange forms with fancy, yet to imagine
> An Antony were nature's piece, 'gainst fancy
> Condemning shadows quite.

Shakespeare, at a profound level, associated dreams with stage representation, since "shadows" for him are both roles for actors, and forms appearing in dreams, or any semblance of fancy, as in "a shadow like an Angel." Of all Shakespearean dreams, probably the most memorable is that of the Duke of Clarence in *Richard III*, replete as it is with the dramatic irony that portends his imminent, grotesque murder: He will be drowned in "a butt of Malmsey," a barrel of wine, to finish him off after being stabbed. His dream, for its length, may be the most comprehensive and universal in all literature, and acutely exemplifies many of the crucial associative links between prophecy and dream. It opens with his escape from the Tower, after which he finds himself on a ship bound for Burgundy, in the company of his monstrous brother, the Duke of Gloucester, who will become King Richard III. The dream, as Shakespeare assumes his audience to know, thus recalls the earlier voyage to Burgundy by Clarence and Gloucester, when they sought safety after the murder of their father, the head of the House of York. Uncannily accurate in its forebodings, Clarence's dream pierces the hypocrisy of Gloucester, which Clarence consciously is incapable of doing. Gloucester "stumbles," the wretched Clarence attempts to steady him, and Clarence is pushed overboard in recompense. And then his great vision begins:

> O Lord, methought what pain it was to drown!
> What dreadful noise of waters in my ears!
> What sights of ugly death within my eyes!
> Methoughts I saw a thousand fearful wracks;
> A thousand men that fishes gnaw'd upon;
> Wedges of gold, great anchors, heaps of pearl,
> Inestimable stones, unvalued jewels,
> All scatt'red in the bottom of the sea:
> Some lay in dead men's skulls, and in the holes
> Where eyes did once inhabit, there were crept
> (As 'twere in scorn of eyes) reflecting gems,
> That woo'd the slimy bottom of the deep,
> And mock'd the dead bones that lay scatt'red by.

What are the gold wedges and precious stones doing in this passage? At the least they represent Clarence's condition of not dying, his "near-death experience" in today's jargon, and ironically they are an emblem of his inability to die at and by his own will:

... and often did I strive
To yield the ghost; but still the envious flood
Stopp'd in my soul, and would not let it forth
To find the empty, vast, and wand'ring air,
But smother'd it within my panting bulk,
Who almost burst to belch it in the sea.

There are intimations here that Clarence cannot drown by water, and the grim image of "burst to belch" also hints at his death by immersion in wine, a weird parody of the communion sacrament. Next Clarence finds himself in a Hades become a hell, where he encounters the Prince of Wales, whom he helped murder. This "shadow like an angel, with bright hair/ Dabbled in blood" shrieks aloud for the Furies to take his murderer, and the howling cries of these diabolic avengers literally awaken Clarence to the scene of his actual murder. The occult element is the double drowning, spared by water yet immolated by wine, and Clarence's narrative is itself an interpretation of his own prophetic dream, indeed Clarence's "dream of interpretation." Schopenhauer, once said, doubtless ironically, that "everyone, while he dreams, is a Shakespeare." If we unpack the irony, we confront the key element in the nature of dreams, and of dream interpretation, which is the process of association. I have cited Clarence's dream at such length because it demonstrates that Shakespeare, rather than Freud, is the seer of association as the basis both of the dream and of its analysis. This was curiously transformed by Freud into the method of so-called free association that he imposed upon his patients. Freud resolutely denied any link between the associationist psychology of the eighteenth century and his free association, but he himself had translated John Stuart Mill, whose psychology remained associationist, and permanently absorbed Mill's idea of object representation, which derived from John Locke, the ultimate source of associationism. Most simply, according to Freud, all dreams depend upon associative chains of imagery and ideas, fantastic modifications upon empirical data. Ideas and images, whether in series or simultaneously, seem to call one another up quite automatically. Memory, like habit, is a repetitive mode that attaches ideas in a fixed way either to pain or pleasure. Habits and memories refine down to intuitive forebodings, helping to provide the anxious dimensions of dreams. Later in this chapter, I will show Freud rejecting the prophetic function of dreams, but then pragmatically readmitting the dreamer's future through free association, as well as through the phenomenon of telepathy, which Freud rationally rejected yet never could quite dismiss from his own uncanniest intuitions.

Is our Western habit (by no means universal) of regarding dreams as illusory or fanciful a truly pragmatic stance? Wendy Doniger (O'Flaherty), a great scholar of the ancient Indian religious traditions, provides a marvelous corrective to our condescensions in her *Dreams, Illusion and Other Realities* (1984). Doniger shows that Indian medicine and philosophy refuse our distinction between meaningful images within the dream, and the question of the reality of dreams as contrasted to the empirical world. According to the *Atharva Veda*, in Doniger's account, "the dreamer can dream the dreams of other people; that is, he can have dreams that symbolize the future events that will happen not to him but to his family." In a culture where the self overlaps more easily than in ours, dreams appear to overlap also, and yet shared dreams (in the literal sense) occur among us also, whether by telepathy or through other bonds we do not yet comprehend. Plato, and all Neoplatonic tradition after him, challenged the hard position of Heraclitus, which was that awake we share one reality, but dreaming we go into a purely private world. Socrates, in the *Dialogues*, breaks down the distinction between dreaming and waking; we cannot know "whether we are asleep and our thoughts are a dream, or whether we are awake and talking with each other in a waking condition." Indeed, for Socrates, most of us are essentially dreaming all the time, and only a few philosophers are actually awake. Plato, perhaps more than Socrates, feared the dream, with its more-than-rational energies, but his respect for dreams influenced his later, Neoplatonist followers (the Sufis included) more than his wariness concerning the visions of the night. Doniger points out that many Indian sages agree more with Plato than with Freud:

> We *can* apply scientific laws to the contents of dreams, *pace* Freud, but not to the process of the dream—to the question of whether or not it is a dream, of whether or not we are awake.

Doniger follows the Hindu sages in granting "psychological reality" to the dream; as we will see, Freud precisely refuses to do just that. Yet, as Doniger adds, the Indian emphasis is more upon shared dreams than on private ones, which may well be illusions. Shared dreams of love that lead to actual relationships are much less Western phenomena than they are Indian. Still, there are generic or well-nigh universal dreams in most cultures, if not in all, though they lack the unsettling, telepathic quality of the Indian dreams in which two potential lovers simultaneously invoke one another. Doniger is very shrewd in saying that, in our own culture, in a psychoanalytic context, such telepathy is induced by the analyst's manipulation (perhaps unconsciously) of transference, which makes the analyst into what, in India, might be considered a medium or even a god. Dreaming a dream simultaneously dreamed by another, though distinctly odd in our social "reality," is a crucial element in many traditions, including Indian and Australian aboriginal. Here we reach a frontier where Freud himself uneasily turned aside, since we can neither prove nor disprove (as yet) the reality of shared dreams.

Doniger ends her marvelous book by pondering the Indian proclivity to believe the rather charming notion that our cosmos is at once the dream of God and the body of God, essentially the idea called *maya*. Though she is certainly accurate in giving India primacy in this exaltation of the dream, something like it has a strong place in Western Gnosis, as I will illustrate in chapter 4. The dream belongs to an angelic realm in Christian Gnosticism, Islamic Sufism, and Jewish Kabbalah. Between the dream aspect of that realm and ourselves, as the Millennium approaches, the great blocking agent is Freud, to whose dream book I now turn.

SIGMUND FREUD'S DREAM BOOK

It could be argued that *The Interpretation of Dreams,* published late in 1899, has been the most influential single intellectual work of the twentieth century. Unfortunately, Freud's great book is marred by its scientism, or making a fetish out of science, yet even this flaw has not prevented its lasting triumph as an interpretive model, and as a kind of spiritual autobiography, a confessional masterpiece. Finished initially when Freud was forty-four, the book underwent nearly forty more years of revision, and defies even the most detailed and responsible of commentaries. I particularly recommend *Freud's Wishful Dream Book* by Alexander Welsh (1994), a recent study that is a wonder of clarity and balance. Welsh emphasizes that the positive achievement, despite Freud's period-piece mere scientism, and a tendency for psychoanalytic ideology to prevail over truthfulness, remains indisputable in two areas: the notion that each of us is bound by the contingencies of personal history, and a very persuasive method of analyzing personal narrative. Neither of these contributions is what Freud most strongly asserted he was offering, which was a universal theory of dreams.

A dream, despite Freud, is by no means always the disguised fulfillment of a repressed wish, and Freud's obsessive insistence on this formulation was rightly judged by the philosopher Ludwig Wittgenstein to be only a rather muddled speculation. Even the clearest speculation would have more in common with myth than with science, and psychoanalysis certainly was precisely what Wittgenstein called it: "a powerful mythology." Still, every theory of dreams has proved to be a mythology, and Freud's at least is the most powerful of all. Freud's ambition was prophetic; though intensely secular, he longed to be the prophet of a new revelation, possibly even of a new Jewishness, though hardly of a new Judaism. In a marvelous irony, he intended to establish his status as a prophet by denying to dreams any prophetic function whatsoever. This oldest of human associations with the dream died hard even in Freud, since in the broad sense he owed everything to the Jewish passion for interpretation, which found a necessary paradigm for prophetic dream interpretation in the prophetic aspects of scriptural interpretation.

I have indicated previously the oddity of Freud's ambivalent stance towards telepathy, since he opposes it on empirical grounds but secretly was captivated by its possibilities. Ernest Jones, Freud's hagiographer, devotes an entire chapter to his master's "occultism." Jung of course firmly believed in the occult, and so did Freud's disciple, the great Sándor Ferenczi. Since Jones was very hardheaded indeed, his chapter on Freud and such matters as telepathy and clairvoyance is a most uncomfortable performance, culminating however in a just assessment:

The wish to believe fought hard with the warning to disbelieve. They represented two fundamental features in his personality, both indispensable to his achievements. But here he was truly wracked; little wonder he bewailed that the topic "perplexed him to distraction."

I suggest that Freud's perplexity sprang from the same conflict in him that always prevented his composition of a much-promised essay on the counter-transference. Telepathy in Freud's circle was a phenomenon that generally took place between male analyst and female patient, the domain of the pseudo-erotic or false connection of the analytic transference. Freudian praxis supposed that the patient was to experience an illusory falling-in-love with her doctor, who then was to exploit this eros for therapeutic purposes only. Counter-transference, or the analyst's emotive relation to the patient, is the land mine of psychoanalysis, though in Freud himself its truly fearful form is best exposed in *Totem and Taboo,* where the totem-father, having appropriated all the women of the tribe, is at last slain and devoured by his jealous, rival sons. Unlike Ferenczi and so many others among the disciples, Freud was not particularly susceptible to being seduced by his female patients, but he had a dread, perhaps only partly conscious, that endless Jungs and Adlers would rise up against him in the primal horde he had fathered. Telepathy and clairvoyance, particularly in foretelling dreams, thus took on both their menace and their allure from the superheated context of transference and counter-transference.

In a lecture entitled "Dreams and the Occult," Freud asked his auditors "to notice that it was not dreams that seemed to teach us something about telepathy, but the interpretation of the dreams, the psychoanalytic treatment of them." This is perhaps only another expression of Freud's lack of respect or affection for dreams, as opposed to his passion for his own interpretations. Dreams, dark and irrational, even magical to so many of us, were to Freud quite clear in their thought, even though that clarity had suffered repression. Richard Wollheim, Freud's most lucid exegete, remarks that the element of wish *in* dreams is not expressed *by* dreams (according to Freud) so that the disguise, or dream-work, results from the wish's repression well *before* it slips into the dream. This allows Freud to insist more persuasively that the hidden dream-thought is identical with the severe rationalizations of his incessant interpretations. Yet the dream narratives that constitute Freud's evidence are either his own, or they emerge from the erotic pressure-cooker of his patients' transferences *to him*. A grand charismatic, with extraordinary, well-nigh hypnotic powers of suggestion, Freud must have recognized, sometimes "unconsciously," that he had a marked telepathic or clairvoyant effect upon his patients. Their dreams, poor things, may have been their own, but the *telling* of their dreams was already Freudian, even before interpretation began. Freud's free associations became his patients' compelled associations, and an authentic occult relation governed the analytic session.

Prophetic dreams haunted Freud, because for him the deepest wish fulfillment had to be his fully accomplished intellectual ambition. *The Interpretation of Dreams* finds it necessary to tell us that, when Freud was born, an aged peasant woman proclaimed that a great man had come into the world. Freud modestly observes that such prophecies are plentiful, but he does not deceive himself or us. Though the greatest of demystifiers, surpassing Nietzsche and Marx, Freud almost allows himself to hint that he is a secular messiah. His ultimate motive as a dream interpreter was to mask his own ambition, the mask being "science." This obsessive scientism, which now mostly distresses us, was also a defense against anti-Semitism. Freud hoped to ward off accusations that his psychoanalysis was a purely Jewish mode of interpretation. Yet psychoanalysis was and is a shamanism; its affiliations with occultism or parapsychology are far more authentic than its supposed links to biology, as a discipline. Freud kept hoping that psychoanalysis would make a contribution to biology, but this was an absurd wish. Though it is an ideology that exalts fact, Freud's creation is a mythology, reared upon the central myth of the drives of love and death. In the longest perspective its deepest affinities are with the pre-Socratic shaman Empedocles, whose vision of incessant strife emerges again in the Freudian tragic view of a civil war in the individual psyche. The darkest Freudian insight, mythological but wholly persuasive, is that each of us is her or his own worst enemy, an insight that I strongly suspect that Freud owed most strongly to the tragic protagonists of Shakespeare.

It seems initially odd, even to me, that a book about angels, the "near-death experience," and the Millennium should have to deal with the rationalistic and rationalizing Sigmund Freud, but the dream is an inevitable context as analogue for the realms of angels, astral bodies, and messianic expectations. For me, and I think for most of us, Freud attempted a remarkably successful (though impermanent) usurpation of the dream world, particularly in the West. Ultimately, I prefer Valentinus the Gnostic, Ibn 'Arabi the Sufi, and Moses Cordovero the Kabbalist to Freud as an authority upon the interpretation of dreams, but I believe we must go *through* Freud in order to get back to what he so persuasively rejected, which in the first place was the authority or value of the dream *in itself*. In some respects, the dream constituted for Freud not so much what he called it, the royal road to the unconscious, but a royal road away from the unconscious, in the older, primal, indeed Gnostic sense of the original Abyss.

Against Freud's dream book, nearly everything has been said by partisans of all persuasions. I think one can admit every objection, and still find the work a magnificence, provided that one dismisses, once and for all, the unhappy assertion that Freud was a scientist. As Francis Crick archly remarks, Freud was a physician with a remarkable literary style. So of course was the seventeenth-century Sir Thomas Browne, author of the *Religio Medici*, but Freud had more than style. He was a great writer, as much a novelist of the self as Saint Augustine and Dante, as much a major moral essayist as Montaigne and Emerson, and a considerable dramatist, though not quite in the range of Molière and Ibsen, let alone of that mortal god, William Shakespeare. Freud's true place is as the rival of the central writers of the twentieth century: Proust, Joyce, Kafka, Beckett, Pirandello, and their handful or so of peers. Freud wished to be Darwin but, as Alexander Welsh shows, had more authentic affinities with Dickens.

I have made clear already that between the sages—Vedantic, Talmudic, Sufi, and others—on dreams, and Freud, I unhesitatingly have learned to follow the sages. And yet Freud's is the largest, more-or-less rationalized theory of dream interpretation ever ventured. With the Millennium approaching, we are long out of the Age of Freud, but he is still the best, last representative of an empiricism open to imaginative speculation that we have, and his presence in this book is intended to be anti-thetical to the Gnosis, which, for me, best explains the persis-tence of the grand images of angels, dream prophecies, near-death astral-body appearances, and other omens of the Millennium. Freud is not what he said he was, or what we may have thought he was, but who else can we turn to as our Plato, our Montaigne, our Emerson?

Ludwig Wittgenstein, far more than Martin Heidegger the enlightened philosopher of our era, manifested what I would term an accurate ambivalence towards Freudian theory, which he regarded not even as theory but as *speculation:* "something prior even to the formation of an hypothesis." Wisdom, which Wittgenstein found in Tolstoy, he could not locate in Freud, which I find surprising, since Freud vies with Proust as the wis-dom writer of our search for lost time. Wittgenstein, an in-tensely spiritual consciousness, was looking for an older wisdom than Freud *seemed* to exemplify, perhaps a folk sagacity. Never-theless, Freud troubled Wittgenstein, even as he troubled Franz Kafka and Gershom Scholem, both of whom overtly rejected him, and as he troubled Borges and Nabokov, both of whom were positively violent and uncivil concerning the founder of psychoanalysis. In a much quieter and more persuasive way, Wittgenstein's skepticism was more interesting:

> Freud's theory of dreams. He wants to say that what-ever happens in a dream will be found to be connected with some wish which analysis can bring to light. But this proce-dure of free association and so on is queer, because Freud never shows how we know where to stop—where is the

right solution. Sometimes he says that the right solution, or the right analysis, is the one which satisfies the patient. Sometimes he says that the doctor knows what the right solution or analysis of the dream is whereas the patient doesn't: the doctor can say that the patient is wrong.

The reason why he calls one sort of analysis the right one, does not seem to be a matter of evidence. Neither is the proposition that hallucinations, and so dreams, are wish fulfillments. Suppose a starving man has an hallucination of food. Freud wants to say the hallucination of anything requires tremendous energy: it is not something that could normally happen, but the energy is provided in the exceptional circumstances where a man's wish for food is overpowering. This is a *speculation*. It is the sort of explanation we are inclined to accept. It is not put forward as a result of detailed examination of varieties of hallucinations.

Wittgenstein is even more suggestive upon Freud's *Freier Einfall* ("free association"):

What goes on in *Freier Einfall* is probably conditioned by a whole host of circumstances. There seems to be no reason for saying that it must be conditioned only by the sort of wish in which the analyst is interested and of which he has reason to say that it must have been playing a part. If you want to complete what seems to be a fragment of a picture, you might be advised to give up trying to think hard about what is the most likely way the picture went, and instead simply to stare at the picture and make whatever dash first comes into your mind, without thinking. This might in many cases be very fruitful advice to give. But it would be astonishing if it *always* produced the best results. What dashes you make, is likely to be conditioned by everything that is going on about you and within you. And if I knew one of the factors present, this could not tell me with certainty what dash you were going to make.

What Wittgenstein implies is that there are many varieties of free association, and so many kinds of dreams: there is no *essence* of dreaming. "A powerful mythology" was Wittgenstein's final judgment upon all of Freud, including the Freudian interpretation of dreams. In justice to Freud I contrast Richard Wollheim to Wittgenstein, as Wollheim, himself a distinguished analytical philosopher, makes the best case for a Freud who is not primarily a speculator. Wollheim asks: what is the evidence for the Freudian theory of dreams, keeping the theory to its essence: that a dream is a disguised fulfillment of a suppressed or repressed wish, and that the element of disguise is explained by Freud's central idea: "the dream-work." A dream-report has a "manifest content" that we remember, but there is also a "latent content" or "dream-thoughts" which by "the dream-work" are made into the manifest content. "Dream-work," certainly one of Freud's most powerful myths or metaphors, goes on through four processes: condensation, displacement, representation, and secondary revision. Condensation is simply the shrinking of latent into manifest content. Displacement is substitution through association, so as to produce disguise. Representation is just the weaving of thoughts into images. But "secondary revision" is yet another strong (and rather dubious) Freudian myth, since it involves the mind's effort to reshape the dream into "intelligibility" (in Freud's own sense). Even Freud began to feel the overkill of this self-serving metaphor, and eventually he withdrew it from his account of the dream-work.

Freud's defense of "the dream-work," as Wollheim shows, depends completely upon another Freudian metaphor, "the censorship," an agency in the mind later to be called the super-ego, and which compels dreams to disguise their real designs. Wollheim rightly sees that Freud tried to save his dream theory by equating dreams with neurotic symptoms, or at least seeing them as strong analogues. Before one is tempted to dismiss Freud for his arbitrariness here, it is best to turn to Philip Rieff, another classic expositor of Freud:

> The inclusiveness of Freud's idea of a symptom should be kept in mind: ultimately all action is symptomatic. There are "normal" symptoms, like the dream, as well as somatic symptoms like a facial tic or a paralyzed leg.

For Freud, all action is symptomatic, because everything has happened already; all action is in the past and there never can be anything utterly new. What happened to one as an infant utterly overdetermines the entire subsequent course of one's existence. That is a very dark view, difficult to accept, and hard to refute. There is for Freud no "white noise"; everything has a meaning, or at least once *had* a meaning. So overdetermined a view of human life has its tragic intensity and its dignity; it possesses also considerable limitations. One sees why Freud chose the interpretation of dreams as his first great battlefield; whatever dreams were to be for him, they had to be insulated from the future, from the unexpected. Everything already was in the past; nothing new of consequence could come upon us. We never should forget that, for Freud, dream interpretation is valid *only in the context of his own therapy.* His therapy has failed, except insofar as it has rejoined the ancient, charismatic praxis of shamanism. By Freud's own standards, then, his mythology of the dream-work is now only a period piece: brilliant, antiquated, speculative rather than scientific. I venture now that Freud's lasting contribution as a dream interpreter is not therapeutic or even narrative, but inheres only in the high quality of his theory's resistance to the immemorial traditions of prophetic dream interpretation. Doubtless, angels are symptoms in the broadest Freudian sense, and what I seek to determine in this book is: symptomatic of what?

PROPHECY AND DREAMS

In his turn away from Judaic dream interpretation—Biblical, Talmudic, Kabbalistic—Freud turned also from all the ancient traditions that linked foretelling and the dream. What was dismissed crept back under the heading of "telepathy," which for Freud was allied to the uncanny and the demonical. Overtly, Freud never wavered in his stance against prophetic dreams, which he expressed with classical elegance as early as 1899:

> Thus the creation of a dream after the event, which alone makes prophetic dreams possible, is nothing other than

a form of censoring, which enables the dream to make its way into consciousness.

Warning his followers away from any alliance with occultists, in 1934 Freud restated his principles:

> Psychoanalysts are fundamentally unreconstructed mechanists and materialists, even though they refuse to strip the mind and the soul of their as yet undetected qualities. They study occult material only because they hope that this would enable them to eliminate once and for all the creations of the human wish from the realm of material reality.

Aside from the unlovely, continual activity of orthodox American Freudians as automobile mechanics of the psyche (lift up the hood, clean out the carburetor, send the human machine back to workaday, ordinary misery), this passage also prophesies the continued analytical smugness concerning "the realm of material reality," or the way things are. Freud himself fought a worthier war, against what he termed the greatest of narcissistic illusions: "the omnipotence of thought," or mind over matter. Parapsychology, whatever validity it may or may not have, did not impress Freud. His exegete, Philip Rieff, follows the lesson of the master in a dismissal that Freud would have enjoyed:

> Among its more extreme proponents, parapsychology is a kind of religion, and, indeed, raises the same ultimate promise as our historic Western religions: that, after all, we never quite die. . . .

The ultimate narcissism refuses death, and Freud's one vestige of Platonism was his worship of the Reality Principle, or coming to terms with the necessity of dying. The "psychology of the unconscious" had to be the explanation for telepathy, clairvoyance, and all similar phenomena.

To dismiss is not to explain, and Freud himself certainly had his own mass of private superstitions, many of them at least as uncanny as telepathy. We have seen how much his own dogma of dream interpretation evades, and I suggest that the wilderness of "free association" in conjunction with the abyss of the analytical transference provides ample space for the accommodation of parapsychology. Free association inevitably calls up sexuality, and the transference is nothing but the summoning of an artificial eros that soon enough turns real, at least on the patient's part. The sexual or erotic future is nearly always an element, however displaced, in our secularized versions of prophetic dreams. Some ideal, future partner seems to haunt our visions of futurity.

We do not know what future partners haunted Freud, but whatever telepathy meant to Freud the dream interpreter, nearly a full century ago, its current significance is now rather different. The influence of dreams upon Freud himself was, as I have shown, largely repressed or evaded by him, though his dream book now seems a paean to his own enormous ambitions. Personal foretelling in or by the dream is one of the underplots of his masterwork, and the occult or telepathic aspect of that foretelling is a considerable element in it.

How could it be otherwise? For thousands of years, every culture on earth had relied upon prophetic dreams and some version of angelic interpretation. Shakespeare abounds in such dreams; his plays scarcely could be what they are without riddling and prophetic intimations, of which I have offered here the dream of poor Clarence in *Richard III* as representative of many others. But for Shakespeare, everything was not already in the past; change and significant action were still to come. While for Freud, dreams can only rehearse past sorrows; *there is nothing to foretell*. Prophecy had ceased in Israel, as well as everywhere else, and Freud's "science" is the seal of the prophets; it is like the Koran, or the New Testament, which renders further dreams superfluous. *The Interpretation of Dreams* was published in December 1899, but was postdated to 1900, so as to inaugurate a new century. Freud was enormously successful; the twentieth century belonged to psychoanalysis. In the twenty-first century, we will consult him on many matters, seeking wisdom, even as we search Montaigne, Emerson, and Nietzsche, his peers. But we will turn elsewhere, as I do now, if we quest for an authority on the prophetic element in dreams. Freud never ceased to see the dream as an agonist, but an opponent weaker than himself. The dream is itself an interpreter, to be overcome by the True Interpreter, Freud. For Freud, the dream is the Angel of Death, and Freud is Jacob (his actual father's name), wrestling until daybreak so as to become Israel, and then depart, limping on his hip. "But it is no sin to limp," Freud/Israel genially remarked in a letter, triumphant at having usurped dream interpretation, for his time.

The Talmudic adage that dreams follow the mouth, that is, their interpreter's mouth, is a very dangerous principle, and the Talmud understood it as such. God sent messengers to us in dreams, but not all dream-angels were from God, since some were demons. If you believed, as the Talmudists and Kabbalists did, that a dream would be prophetic *precisely as it was interpreted*, then acceptance or rejection of an interpretation was not a light matter. But the *first* interpretation made always had a peculiar authority, so the choice of a dispenser of meaning became a crucial one. Joshua Trachtenberg, in his *Jewish Magic and Superstition* (1939), emphasizes direct invocation of the angels in order to solicit both dreams and interpretations from them. The most fascinating dream material in Trachtenberg deals with the counteracting or neutralizing of ominous or bad dreams, by way of "dream fasts" and rituals for converting nightmares into better premonitions, rituals of "overturning."

Divination among the Jews, as among most peoples, generally is fostered by a sense of fatalism, and by the fear of overdetermination, which perhaps is particularly a Jewish phenomenon. Traditional Judaism at once affirmed determinism and free will, as Trachtenberg notes, a very strained situation, but common to Christianity and Islam as well. Howsoever free even the most secular among us feel we are of mere superstition, we may nevertheless find ourselves turning, quite involuntarily, to the reading of omens. Divination, in the widest sense, is necessarily the subject of this book, since I seek to read some of our signs at the end of an age. Magical divination and necromancy do not much move me, but that there is a relation between dreams and prophecy I do not doubt, following in this the most exalted of traditions. The *Zohar,* in an immensely intricate passage on prophetic dreams (I, 183a–183b), tells us that God made many different levels in such dreams, so many that they cannot be revealed directly even to true prophets but must be seen through the "mirror that does not shine," that is to say, the *Shekhinah,* the female indwelling presence of God in the world. The *Shekhinah* is hardly to be thought of as passive; her massive strength is that she reflects all the colored lights that emerge from all of the *sefirot,* all of the emanations or powers or potencies of God. Gabriel, according to the *Zohar,* exercises authority over prophetic dreams, but only theoretically, since unlike Muhammad, the Kabbalist visionary pragmatically deals not with Gabriel but with the *Shekhinah* herself.

David Bakan, in his stimulating but certainly disputable *Sigmund Freud and the Jewish Mystical Tradition* (1958), suggests that the *Shekhinah,* an image at once divine, maternal, and altogether sexual, may have informed Freud's enlarged understanding of the nature of sexuality as "a complex metaphor in which all human meanings are somehow involved." I myself suspect that Shakespeare, with whom Freud was obsessed, was a much likelier source for the metaphor than the *Zohar* could be, but Bakan seems to me correct in observing that Freud's "free association" is closer to the *Zohar*'s freedom from all literalism than it is to the stricter associative techniques of the Talmud. Even if, as seems likely to me, Freud had not the slightest interest in Kabbalah, it is Kabbalah, and Sufism, that for me provide the way back from Freud's blockage of prophetic interpretation of the dream. I cannot see a better principle for prophetic interpretation than the great conceptual image of the *Shekhinah,* whose power of "reflection" embraces every possible meaning of that term. Gershom Scholem, in his definitive study of the *Shekhinah* (most easily available in his *On the Mystical Shape of the Godhead,* 1991), says that Kabbalah created a new understanding of the *Shekhinah:*

> In this world of *Sefiroth,* each of which can be viewed as a hypothesis of a particular facet of God, the *Shekhinah* receives its new meaning as the tenth and final *Sefirah.* The crucial factor in its new status is unquestionably its feminine character, which, as mentioned above, is not found in any pre-Kabbalistic source, but which now absorbs everything capable of such an interpretation in biblical and rabbinic literature. This presentation of the *Shekhinah* as female element—simultaneously mother, bride, and daughter—within the structure of the godhead constitutes a very meaningful step, with far-reaching consequences, one which the Kabbalists attempted to justify by Gnostic interpretation. It is not surprising that the opponents of Kabbalah reacted to this idea with great suspicion. The enormous popularity enjoyed by this new mythic understanding of the concept is illustrated precisely by the fact that it filtered down in the form of confused, apologetic distortions in which the *Shekhinah* was identified and compared with the Divine Providence itself. This fact is undisputable proof that the Kabbalists here touched upon a fundamental and primal need, uncovering one of the perennial religious images latent in Judaism as well.

I think that the deepest insight of this new vision, as Scholem says elsewhere, is "that the form of each and every individual thing is preformed in the *Shekhinah.*" That certainly includes dreams and returns us to Freud's ambivalent stance against prophetic dreams. If all dreams are reflected from the *Shekhinah* (or, as the Sufis said, from Fatima, daughter of the Prophet, or from the Angel Christ, as the Christian Gnostics said), then dreams cannot simply be rearrangements of the past. It is both pragmatic and shrewd of the mystics that they affirm the paradox that our dreams are less individual than we are. We die solitary deaths, but dream communal dreams, which is the true subject of this book, as subsequent chapters shall adumbrate. What the *Shekhinah* or Fatima or the Angel Christ gives in the dream ultimately is the image of the astral body, a man or woman all light. Our "near-death experiences" are simply the prophetic dream proper, or telepathic phenomena in the mode that both distressed and fascinated Freud.

Freud could not resolve his tension concerning telepathic dreams. If they *were* overdetermined symptoms of a single individual only, then they would have to be remarkably more isolated than are the grand, universal Freudian mythologies: the drives, the mechanisms of defense, the frontier concepts such as the bodily ego. Freud's greatest power is to persuade us that we are lived by forces beyond our wills, and by desires that we may never recognize, and by images that we have internalized. The allure of the myth of the dream-work vanishes when we attempt to assimilate it to so compulsive a psychic cosmos. Freud wants it both ways: we are lived by others, yet not dreamed by others. By granting relative autonomy to the dreamer, Freud wants to make each of us more of a poet than an actor, more Shakespeare writing Clarence's dream than the wretched Clarence suffering the narration of it. Yet Freud deeply fears that we are dreamed by others, or as tradition would say, by the angel, the other, the alter ego. If there is dream-work, then all the ancients were right: it is the work of angels. By placing everything except our deaths firmly in the past, Freud violates the deep human truth of the cosmological image of the *Shekhinah:* she necessarily reflects future life as well as the necessity of dying.

Something desperate in Freud caused him to insist that "a dream without condensation, distortion, dramatization, above all without wish fulfillment, does not deserve this name." If you wish to exclude prophetic dreams from the category of dream, then what are you to do with them? Thought transference between dreamers is not altogether different from psychoanalytical transference: in both phenomena, everything depends upon interpretation. Freud should have brooded upon Nietzsche's eternal question: "Who is the interpreter, and what power does he or she attempt to gain over the text?" Ken Frieden remarks, "With the neurotic transference securely redirected towards cure, Freud neglects its role in the handling of dreams and ascribes an almost exclusively cognitive function to dream interpretation." And yet what is psychoanalysis anyway if it does not seek to improve the patient's future, by suggesting interpretations that will work so as to both prophesy and alter a future that will, at the least, improve the past.

Freud absolutely declined to see that *to interpret is to prophesy.* Dream-work, even in the Freudian sense, manifests powers that necessarily transcend the psyche of the individual dreamer. What was Freud to do, confronted by transcendental entities? The most remarkable dream narrated in Freud's book is the uncanny dream of the burning child. A father, whose child has just died, himself falls asleep in another room, while an old man keeps vigil with the dead child. In the father's dream, the child comes to him and says: "Father, don't you see that I am burning?" Waking up from his dream, the father enters the next room to discover that the old man has fallen asleep, and so has failed to see and prevent a candle from setting the dead child's clothes on fire.

Freud interprets this poignant vision as the father's wish fulfillment, bringing the child back to life in much the same extremity as Lear holding the dead Cordelia in his arms. It hardly required the French mystagogue Jacques Lacan to indicate that Freud's careful minimalism here is insupportable, and unworthy of the moral and aesthetic grandeur of the psychoanalytic enterprise. Freud the conquistador blinks at the burning child, who burns with the culpability of the father, of fatherhood itself. No dream in our time could be more prophetic, in the precise sense of requiring, demanding the prophetic interpretation that Freud refuses it. For the burning child is the astral body, and not to read him as a prophetic image is to miss him. We cannot know that the child is burning, so we must imagine it, or rely upon the father's authority. But it is in that imagining, in that choice of reliances, that we ourselves are compelled to prophesy. Freud's dream of the burning child is a parable of limitations, of the refusal of telepathic possibilities, which nevertheless stand out even upon the surface of the dream. No father can fail to respond to "Don't you see that I am burning?" At the furthest limit of his rationalized usurpation of interpretive authority, Freud scandalously refuses to interpret, because he will not accept the office of a prophet.

CHAPTER 3
NOT DYING

THE "NEAR-DEATH EXPERIENCE"

Most of our contemporary celebrations of the "near-death experience" are directly indebted to Raymond A. Moody, Jr.'s *Life After Life* (1976), a "sweetly reasonable" survey of about 150 testimonies from ordinary citizens who asserted that they had returned from near death, bearing benign intimations of immortality. "Near-death experience" was Moody's own phrase, meant to embrace not only those who revived after being pronounced clinically dead, but also survivors of accidents or of extreme danger. "What is it like to die?" is the question that opens Moody's rather cheerful little book, which proceeds to answer with a fairly comprehensive list. In each of these headings the first term is Moody's and the second is mine:

1. Ineffability, or Inexpressibility

This appears to mean a paucity of vocabulary on the part of the near-deathers; why Moody assumed that the experience was ineffable, instead of probing the verbal limitations of his subjects, is not clarified.

2. Hearing the News, or Maldiagnosis

Whether being inaccurately pronounced dead ought to be considered part of "What is it like to die?" seems to me at least questionable, but was not an issue for the credulous Moody.

3. Feelings of Peace and Quiet, or It Doesn't Hurt Anymore

This hardly requires comment, but does raise the problem as to the ambiguities of the "near" in "near death."

4. The Noise: Unpleasant or Pleasant

Most of Moody's informants complained of buzzing, ringing, clicking, roaring, banging, or whistling as they lay dying; others though heard pleasant bells or solacing music. One doesn't know whether or not individual temperaments are responsible for these differences.

5. The Dark Tunnel (or Cave, Well, Trough, Enclosure, Funnel, etc.)

The Moodyers, as they listen to the noise, are rapidly hauled through a darkness, evidently a void of some sort. Moody's metaphor of "the dark tunnel" may owe something to

Jean Cocteau's vivid film *Orpheus;* his interlocutors are in little agreement as to the passageway.

6. *Out of the Body, or Being a Spirit*

Out-of-the-body experience is all but a synonym for the "near-death experience," since it is the center of the phenomenon. The Moody men and women compare their spiritual bodies to mists, clouds, smoke, vapors, etc., and for the most part contemplate their corpses with an admirable detachment, though this frequently is followed by the distress of solitude or isolation. But since the "near-death experience" in contemporary America is careful to remain a Good Thing, such distress is followed quickly by:

7. *Meeting Others, or The Wistfuls*

These amorphous ineffables can be old cronies who have passed on first, or simply anonymous and invisible entities. I myself would want to name them "the Wistfuls" rather than guardian spirits, so as to emphasize their gentle ineffectuality.

8. *The Being of Light, or the Angel Christ*

"The Angel Christ" is my term, not Moody's, but that Gnostic term precisely describes the person of Light whom all the Moodyers encounter, and with whom they communicate telepathically. The function of this Being of Light seems neither saving nor judgmental, but rather only to be the inaugurator of:

9. The Review, or Flashback

This memory process also appears to be educational, rather then judicial, though it tends to be commonplace.

10. The Border, or Limit or Safeguard

Since the Moody "near-death experience" essentially is a comfort and a reassurance, it must feature a limit, reminding us that the "near" is more important than the "death."

11. Coming Back, or Mock Resurrection

Moody's subjects mostly insisted that they were reluctant to come back, having discovered that death was such a Good Thing.

Though Moody adds Telling Others, Effects on Lives, New Views of Death, and Corroboration so as to make up fifteen phases, these final four seem irrelevant to me. In justice to Moody, I quote in full the two paragraphs where he sums up his "near-death experience" as paradigm:

> A man is dying, and as he reaches the point of greatest physical distress, he hears himself pronounced dead by his doctor. He begins to hear an uncomfortable noise, a loud ringing or buzzing, and at the same time feels himself moving very rapidly through a long dark tunnel. After this, he suddenly finds himself outside of his own physical body, but still in the immediate physical environment, and he sees his own body from a distance, as though he is a spectator. He watches the resuscitation attempt from this unusual vantage point and is in a state of emotional upheaval.

After a while he collects himself and becomes more accustomed to his odd condition. He notices that he still has a "body," but one of a very different nature and with very different powers from the physical body he has left behind. Soon other things begin to happen. Others come to meet and to help him. He glimpses the spirits of relatives and friends who have already died, and a loving, warm spirit of a kind he has never encountered before—a being of light—appears before him. This being asks him a question, nonverbally, to make him evaluate his life and helps him along by showing him a panoramic instantaneous playback of the major events of his life. At some point he finds himself approaching some sort of barrier or border, apparently representing the limit between earthly life and the next life. Yet he finds that he must go back to the earth, that the time for his death has not yet come. At this point he resists, for by now he is taken up with his experiences in the afterlife and does not want to return. He is overwhelmed by intense feelings of joy, love, and peace. Despite his attitude, though, he somehow reunites with his physical body and lives.

As a student of influence, particularly in literature and esoteric religion, I suspect that Moody's paradigm has affected not only the curious industry known as "near-death research," but also many "near-death experiences" as well. Moody cites Saint Paul, the *Tibetan Book of the Dead*, and Swedenborg as analogues to his speculations, but I will show much closer analogues in Gnosis: in Christian Gnosticism, Shi'ite Sufism, and Kabbalah. But, alas, just as we have seen a vast difference in spiritual dignity and cognitive force when we contrast our current preoccupation with angels to past visions in that realm, so there is an even starker sense of loss when we compare the astral body or figure of Light in the traditions of Gnosis to the manifestations of the Light in post-Moodyan "near-death experience." But I will provide those contrasts and comparisons in my next chapter, "Gnosis," and in the third section of this chapter, "The Astral Body." Here I need to continue the popular saga of Moodyism, as carried on by a pride of researchers, the most prominent of these being Kenneth Ring, who summarized his findings in *Life at Death* (1980). Though always loyal to Moody, Ring replaces the eleven elements of Moody's model with a much simpler five-stage paradigm: easeful peace, separation from the body, entering the dark void or tunnel, beholding "a magnetic and brilliant light," and finally entering that light. Moody modestly held off from religious prophecy, but Ring has joined the New Age and insists that the survivors of the "near-death.experience" are thereby more advanced human beings than the rest of us. Rather than comment upon this Ringian value judgment, I prefer to cite him at his most interesting:

Moody spoke of a "being of light," and though none of our respondents used this phrase, some seemed to be aware of a "presence". (or "voice") in association with the light. Often, but not always, this presence is identified with God. However this may be, I want to consider what the light represents when it is conjoined with the sense of a presence or with an unrecognized voice.

Here we must, I think, make a speculative leap. I submit that this presence/voice is actually—oneself! It is not merely a projection of one's personality, however, but one's *total self*, or what in some traditions is called the *higher self*. In this view, the individual personality is but a split-off fragment of the total self with which it is reunited at the point of death. During ordinary life, the individual personality functions in a seemingly autonomous way, as though it were a separate entity. In fact, however, it is invisibly tied to the larger self structure of which it is a part. An analogy would be that the individual personality is like a child who, when grown up, completely forgets his mother and then fails to recognize her when they later meet.

As speculation, this is not unconfused, but its interest stems from its Aquarian, or made-in-America, Gnosis. Ring, like his forerunner Moody, is aware of analogues both ancient and esoteric, and yet is held back from understanding the analogues by an odd literalism concerning the "near-death experience," in which again he follows Moody. I call such literalism "odd" because it refuses to confront the absurdity or hopelessness of all our current American embraces by the Light. Those avid for this embrace are desperate for assurances as to immortality, by which they actually mean not dying at all. But even hundreds of thousands of *near*-death experiences of necessity tell us absolutely *nothing* about *after*-death survival, of any kind. Death, one's own death, is alas a rather different affair from even the warmest and most reassuring near-death escapade.

My very own "near-death experience" took place when I was going on sixty; I had ignored, indeed stupidly denied, a bleeding ulcer, and entered Yale–New Haven Hospital, having lost sixty percent of the blood in my Falstaffian body. Before falling asleep in the emergency ward even as many pints of blood began to flow back into me, I made my own pilgrimage to the outer limits, while half-consciously listening to my younger son's comforting remarks, until I crossed the borders of sleep. I did not encounter Moody's eleven elements, or Ring's five stages, but I found myself in something like Jean Cocteau's cinematic near-death realm, *Orpheus,* and rather detachedly wandered about, perhaps a touch less panicky at being lost than customarily I am. There was indeed a rather bright light as I went under, but it was annoying rather than comforting. This certainly seemed a considerably lesser experience than the William Jamesian "Anesthetic Revelation" that I experienced under the sway of nitrous oxide, when I had three impacted wisdom teeth deftly removed by a London dentist, a quarter-century before my ulcerous ordeal. Like so many of James's informants, I had a grand religious revelation, unveiling the secrets of Eternity, and exulted that I was returning to bear the good news, only to discover on coming up out of it that the truth had abandoned me utterly.

I do not mean to deprecate anyone's "near-death experience." Rather I want to suggest that our popular obsession with it is strikingly akin to our current debasement of the angelic world. There is, I am persuaded, a considerable spiritual reality involved in both obsessive concerns, but our commercialization of these matters has ensued in a travesty of ancient verities. To read the scholar Henry Corbin upon the Sufi vision of "the Man of Light" is to encounter a far more challenging and urgent sense of living or dying than emerges from the "researches" of the Moody-Ring industry. Industry it certainly has become, just as the purveyors of angels are a growth item. We now have IANDS (the International Association for Near Death Studies) which offers maroon T-shirts, and features a logo that inter-mixes Moody's tunnel with the Taoist emblem of yin and yang. The quarterly put out is called *Vital Signs;* there are workshops, conventions, study groups, and much else. This sounds rather like a novel by Aldous Huxley or even Evelyn Waugh, but is merely another instance of American millennial hysteria.

I again state that I do not consider anyone's "near-death ex-perience" to be only what one skeptic named as a "toxic psy-chosis," but the exploitation of the phenomenon would be worthy of a major satirist, if only we had one anymore. Be Glad You Nearly Died, the implicit motto of the Moody-Ringers, has a charm to it, but one that vanishes when the members of IANDS endeavor to extract theological or theosophical wisdom from their eleven elements and five stages. Carol Zaleskie, whose *Otherworld Journeys* (1987) is the best-informed and fairest study of near-death matters, concludes her book by say-ing, "Near-death literature is at its best when it is modest and anecdotal; pressed into service as philosophy or prophecy, it sounds insipid." It *is* insipid, even as our current, popular angel narratives are insipid. The Moody-Ringers, like the angel en-thusiasts and the veterans of alien encounters and abductions, are no better equipped to verify and interpret their supposed experiences than Moody and Ring are. I turn to the shamans, permanent professionals of out-of-body experience, whose otherworld journeys are the authentic starting point for under-standing the near-death phenomenon. Nearly dying is our con-temporary halfhearted evasion of Gnosis and its vision of resurrection, or not dying, the vision of the Being of Light that connects Christian Gnosticism, Sufism, and the Kabbalah, vital traditions of visionary experience and its interpretation.

SHAMANISM: OTHERWORLDLY JOURNEYS

All shamanisms depend upon the idea that once there was no barrier between Heaven and earth; the shaman is the person who can break through our limits, and who can achieve the freedom of reopening the way back to larger human powers, now apparently lost. Dream prophecy is one of those powers, and I will return to it later to help explain not so much the origins of shamanism, which as a worldwide phenomenon defies any single account of beginnings, but the specific entry of shamanism into Western tradition. As a word (in Tungus) *shaman* means a sorcerer, one who employs the methods of ecstasy, including out-of-the-body experiences, in order to invoke the world of the spirits.

Ecstatic prophecy, whether in spoken oracles or in dreams and their interpretation, is one of the principal results of spirit invocation, and seems to have been practiced in almost all cultures. E. R. Dodds, in his superb book *The Greeks and the Irrational* (1951), interpreted the classical religion of Apollo as one of ecstatic prophecy, featuring "the blessings of madness." Since archaic Greek dreams were *seen* (rather than "had"), if they were prophetic, then the future actually was visible, generally in the shape of a god, or even of a dead or absent friend substituting for a god. That substitution takes us into the world of the Greek shamans, whose influence Dodds centers upon the distinction between the *psyche,* or "soul," and an "occult self" at first also called *psyche,* but which gradually was named as the *pneuma* ("breath") or the *daemon,* for which we have no adequate equivalent in English.

The occult self was divine in its origins, unlike the soul, which to the Greeks was very much at home in the body. Not so the new self of the shamans, imported into Greece from Thrace, to the north, and so ultimately from barbarous Scythia, into which central Asians had descended. The strife between divine self and natural soul, previously unknown to the Greeks, is crucial to all shamanism, and is a basic element in the Greek shamans Pythagoras and Empedocles, men who were divine or semi-divine, at least to their followers. The mythical Orpheus may have begun as a figure much like Pythagoras and Empedocles, as another shaman who, as Dodds puts it, taught that we have a detachable self, "which by suitable techniques can be withdrawn from the body even during life, *a self which is older than the body and will outlast it*" (my italics).

A self that is the oldest and best part of one, a divine and magical self: this shamanistic belief, which we also call Orphic, seems to me the origin of all Gnosticism—whether Jewish, Christian, or Islamic—and of the secular, Alexandrian Gnosticism called the Hermetic Corpus, which became the foundation for Bruno and other mystagogues of the Italian Renaissance. Shamanism is universal, and this may account for the curious universalism of what normative believers of all ages term "the Gnostic heresy." The phenomena I am addressing in this book—angelicism, prophetic dreams, "near-death experiences," millennial fears, and apocalyptic yearnings—do not manifest themselves now to us as normative but as Gnostic tendencies, though generally in a debased form, not just popularized but also commercialized. At their kernel is the ancient emergence of Gnosticism from shamanism, particularly from the shamanistic occult or magical self. Orpheus may have been only a potent myth, but Empedocles was an actual sage, who denied that the *psyche* was the true, undying self in each of us, and affirmed rather that the *daemon* was our destiny, because it was what was best and oldest in us, and so potentially was divine.

The principal scholarly study, *Shamanism* (1951, 1964), by the late Mircea Eliade, emphasizes that shamans, throughout space and time, originate from initiations that blend pathological illnesses with prophetic dreams, so that we scarcely can distinguish the sickness from the prophecy. Once shamanistic powers are attained, the shamans characteristically undertake otherworldly journeys, to all the heavens and all the hells, in order to carry out their distinctive labors of healing illness, both pathological and physical. Eliade ventures that "the specific element of shamanism is not the embodiment of 'spirits' by the shaman, but the ecstasy induced by his descent to the underworld." That "ecstasy," which is manifested so rarely in our contemporary otherworldly journeys, whether of the "near-death experience" or the "alien abduction" variety, is the authentic mark or stigma not only of the shaman but of the Gnostic of any era or tradition. There is evidently a vital sense in which such shamanistic ecstasy pragmatically is the Gnosis, the knowing in which we become one with what is known. Can we define that ecstasy, and by defining it can we come to understand what otherworldly journeys *ought* to be?

Shamanistic ecstasy comes in a trance condition, which itself is necessary for the shaman's journey. Frequently the trance is drug induced, or at least aided by one intoxicant or another, sometimes by a sacred, hallucinatory mushroom. R. Gordon Wasson and Wendy Doniger O'Flaherty, in their *Soma: Divine Mushroom of Immortality* (1968), identify soma as being, in all likelihood, the fly agaric of northern Eurasia, a bright red mushroom flecked with white spots. The ancient Vedic hymns that celebrate soma and that stand as the origins of Hinduism were gathered together as the *Rig Veda,* more than a thousand poems praising the gods and their achievements. Composed mostly around 1200 B.C.E., the hymns were the work of a people who invaded India from southern Russia, possibly around 1500 B.C.E., presumably bringing their shamanistic culture with them, Soma being the name of one of their gods. These Vedic Indians, who have been the prime people of the subcontinent ever since, worshipped a storm god and divine warrior, Indra, as the chief of deities. Indra, powerful in himself, grew immensely stronger on soma (the mushroom, not the god), or rather a liquor extracted from the mushroom, or from the plant we call wild rue, according to authorities who do not accept the mushroom hypothesis. Soma is regarded in the *Rig Veda* as a cure-all, increasing potency and so life itself.

Scholars of shamanism, Eliade included, tend to employ Siberian shamanism as their archetype, since historically our earliest evidence of shamanistic origins is central Asian, and Siberian praxis seems not to have changed since archaic days.

Shamanistic trance or ecstasy generally has a narcotic element in modern times, and frequently relies upon mushrooms; Eliade surmises that "pure" trance was more truly archaic, and yet the Iranian Sufis, the most spiritual and intellectual of all shamans, followed Vedic precedent in relying upon sacred intoxication, as their marvelous poetic tradition continually demonstrates. The archaic techniques of ecstasy set forth by Eliade actually tend to be more drastic and frightening than mere soma. Whether initiated by mental illness or by weird dreams, shamanism rapidly comes to depend upon otherworldly journeys that may involve the pragmatic preparation of being tortured to death. The high price of freeing the spirit to seek the spirits can be a drastic "liberation" from the body. Resurrection unfortunately demands dying as a precondition, and shamanistic "deaths" do not always require location within quotation marks. I myself always have been puzzled as to why historical Catholicism and its primary Protestant foes, Lutheranism and Calvinism, have shied away from the forty days that the resurrected Jesus spent going about with the disciples, before he ascended again into heaven. I would answer now: Is not the Jesus of the Gnostics and of a multitude of American religionists essentially a shaman? That is why the ancient Valentinian Gnostics and so many Americans alike worship primarily *the resurrected Jesus:* not the Jesus who was tortured to death on the cross, in a terrible ecstasy, but the Jesus who was resurrected in a benign ecstasy, holding earth and heaven open to one another again. The chosen of the resurrected Jesus share this second ecstasy, and worship therefore the most universal of all shamans.

"Near-death experiences," when they are shamanistic, have

little in common with our current American Moody-Ring soft-edged recitals. Though undergone in ecstasy, shamanistic initiation frequently involves death by mutilation, followed by a resurrection that reintegrates the shattered body. What credence can be given to these magical violences that defy the limits of our empirical world? Ecstatic trance can seem a kind of death, convincingly enough, but shamanistic *sparagmos* is clearly something else, which I assume relies upon the persuasive methods of sorcery, or enters realms difficult to apprehend: hyperspace, or the fourth dimension. Wherever or whatever the shaman enters, first in dream and then in reality, whether his own or ours or both, what matters is the otherworldliness of the journey. The shaman travels to heal illness, sometimes of a single person, sometimes of a tribe, yet the healing can be accomplished only after the shaman himself has known the illness, whether derangement or dismemberment. Central to shamanism are its supposed mysteries: flight, levitation, gender transformation, bilocation, and animal and bird incarnations. All these phenomena, however startling, are merely means to the single end of shamanism: restoring the undying self of the dead. Like Hermes the soul raiser, who could lead souls back from Hades as well as to it, the shaman is the pragmatic exemplification of the Heraclitean truth that the way down and the way up are one and the same.

There is no simple relation between dreams and otherworld journeys, whether archaic or modern. Interpenetration of dream-account and quest-narrative is the norm; both are forms of romance, in the technical sense of a marvelous story that depends for its effect upon imperfect knowledge, upon the enchantment of the unencountered. The common ground of shamanistic dreams and voyages is the ultimate human desire: survival in the confrontation with death. Theologians work at doubtless higher levels, but the Jesus of the people, almost everywhere, is the universal shaman. This may not be against the genius of Christianity, but it certainly is against the teaching of Catholicism and the mainline Protestant churches. Resurrection for these does *not* follow the pattern of Jesus, whose ascension in those traditions was viewed as a kind of promissory note for the vast resurrection someday to come, or perhaps more as a first installment. Even Dante, in the arrogant pride of his *Divine Comedy,* does not model his otherworldly voyages upon those of Christ; he seems to have understood his own dark brotherhood with Ulysses better than his commentators do. Popular spiritualism, which long before the New Age had become our urban shamanism, has moved into this gap so curiously left open by Christianity, the gap between Christ's Resurrection and our own.

The shamanism confronted by the contemporary Roman church is best exemplified by Catholic feminists, the authentic shock troops of the New Age. I am not minded to take sides either with the Church or with its feminist rebels, but wish only to indicate the shamanistic (and Gnostic) patterns enacted by these highly successful networkers, who may yet take over much of the American church from within. "Woman Church," the largest of the feminist "liturgical communities," knowingly or not works towards a vision of Jesus the shaman whose tutelary spirit was Mary Magdalene. Ritual androgynization is one of the roots of shamanism; male shamans turn female and female,

male, in what may be a variant upon the shamanistic art of bilo-cation, or being in two distant places simultaneously, appearing in the shape of one gender or the other, or as an animal, or a bird. In Gnosticism, the primal Abyss is called both Foremother and Forefather, and the Gnostic original Adam, Anthropos, is an androgyne. Shamanism, unlike Gnosticism, is not a religion but is a series of modes of ecstasy, some of which may be start-ing points for the experience of Gnosis, for a knowing in which the knower herself is known, a reciprocity of deep self and tutelary spirit. That helps account for the peculiar nature both of shamanistic and of Gnostic otherworldly voyages. It appears to make little difference whether the shaman mounts up to the sky or descends to an underworld. Clambering up a birch tree after sacrificing a horse, the shaman experiences an ecstasy that destroys the distinction between literal and symbolic ascent. Or else the shaman goes down a hole in the earth, navigates through an underground sea, and emerges in the hut of the King of the Dead. Again the attendant ecstasy compounds the literal and the emblematic, so that we cannot be certain what the actual descent was or was not. In the domain of shamanism, the occult self sets the rules, which necessarily are ecstatic and archaic.

Can we distinguish between trance and possession in shamanism? This difficult question is the subject of *Ecstatic Re-ligion: A Study of Shamanism and Spirit Possession* by I. M. Lewis (1971, 1989), in which Lewis argues that trance essen-tially is a state of radically altered consciousness, while posses-sion, which compounds trance with illness, is always a response to cultural conditions, to pressures and expectations that are more than individual. Social anthropology is however itself a great conditioner, and I doubt Lewis's distinction, which depends upon his acceptance of the notion that shamanism arises from social conditions of change and uncertainty. Rather, the evidence is that shamanism was and is universal and primal: always it has been the resource of groups and of individuals who refuse to resign all power to God or the gods. Innate divinity is the center of shamanism as it is of the various offspring of shamanism: Pythagoreanism, Orphism, Gnosticism, Spiritual Enthusiasm. Shamanistic trance is utterly fused with possession by spirits, and I hardly can know what it would mean to call such possession an illness. Whose illness? An immense society governed by psychopharmacology is not privileged to judge ecstatic religion, whether its own or of past time and place. But that returns me to the aspects of shamanism most relevant to this book: prophetic dreams and otherworldly journeys. Our "near-death experiences" are parodies of authentic shamanism precisely because, with very rare exceptions, they have no sense of innate divinity, no conviction that a magical self and not the ordinary Ringian "higher self" is returning to its proper realm. Our dreams and our "out-of-the-body" encounters alike are impoverished by our incapacity for spiritual ecstasy. ✳

It has been noted, by E. R. Dodds and other scholars, that dreams foretelling otherworldly journeys and doctrines of reincarnation almost invariably are associated, as they were both in ancient Greece and in India. The transmigration of souls and prophetic dreams of ascent or descent appear to be different manifestations of the same phenomenon, which is shamanistic initiation, or the dying that must precede resurrection into the powers of a shaman. A dream of dying, even of resurrection, is common enough; few among us are shamans, and yet we dream such dreams. Very rarely though are we spiritually persuaded that an anterior spirit has been reincarnated in us, particularly when the spirit previously had been unknown to us. It is the almost simultaneous initiatory dream and spirit possession that mark out the potential shaman, who then modulates into the ecstatic trance that defines a divinating vocation. A new shaman always must be instructed by an old one, but the choice comes from the spirit, and not from the instructor or the aspirant. I am not much minded to pray that would to God all of our people were shamans (in our current social climate that would result only in still more politicized shamans), but a few marks of authenticity in our supposedly spiritual journeys would not be unwelcome. The particular mark that is now most frequently popularized and commercialized is a being or personage who is all Light, the entity traditionally called "the astral body," to which I turn, seeking as before some evidences of the spirit's survival in a time when mock representations of the spirit abound.

THE ASTRAL BODY: THE ZELEM

Western and Eastern traditions alike abound in variants of the image of "the subtle body," more often than not also termed "the astral body." We can trace—more or less—a likely ambiance for the Western image in Neoplatonism, but the Eastern image is so multiform that it seems always to have been present. The Jungians, being a reductive cult, see the astral body as what their master called the "objective psyche," a notion that is beyond me. I prefer the classical scholar E. R. Dodds, who refers us back to the ancient Greek word *ochema*, a word meaning at once the astral body and the vehicle or chariot, which is compared by Plato in the *Timaeus* to the sowing of each of our souls in a star, by the Demiurge, "as in a chariot" (*ochema*), before some of the souls are placed in bodies upon our earth and some were stored away in the planets. Following both Plato and Aristotle, the Neoplatonist Proclus gave a full exposition of the astral body in his rather dry *Elements of Theology*, in which we are told that this luminous envelope is a bridge between soul and body, and so belongs to everyone. Opposed to this Neoplatonic view is the Hermetist-Gnostic belief that the immortal, astral body is won only through a divinizing Gnosis, and so can be possessed only by an elite of initiates.

These conflicting accounts of the astral body never have been resolved, and persist today in the difference between endless narratives of "near-death experiences" and the rarer visions recorded by a few handfuls of contemporary sages. It is of some importance to note that the older, Neoplatonist view, and its modern survivals, is essentially determinative: Proclus assigns each human soul to the influence of a divine soul resident in one planet or another. There is thus an authentic link between semi-universal "near-death experiences" and astrology, with all of its overdeterminations. The Hermetic-Gnostic initiatory astral body is quite another phenomenon and reached its fullest development in Sufism and in Kabbalah, before its survival, in debased form, in modern spiritualism and occultism. The indispensable commentator on the astral body in Sufism is of course Henry Corbin, whose acute sense of a reality halfway between the empirical and divine worlds is the principal influence upon me, here as elsewhere in this book.

Essentially we may call the astral body by its alternate names of the "body to come," or the "Resurrection Body." The Iranian Sufis excelled in descriptions of their visions of "the Man of Light," the "new body," or "Adam of your being." This Resurrection Body is at once your true ego, or self, and your alter ego, or angelic counterpart, a conjunction that we have encountered before. Corbin remarks that "in all cases it refers to that same world in which the liberated soul, whether in momentary ecstasy or through the supreme ecstasy of death, meets its archetypal 'I,' its alter ego, or celestial Image, and rejoices in the felicity of that encounter." Corbin's "in all cases" is precise: the "momentary ecstasy" belongs to the Gnostic adept, while the "ecstasy" of death is a terrible universal, thus again illustrating the two aspects of the astral body.

The greatest Sufi authority on the Resurrection Body was Shaikh Ahmad Ahsa'i, who died in 1826, and who developed fundamental ideas of Avicenna, the great Persian philosopher of Islam in the eleventh century. Avicenna, in his "visionary recitals," argued for what he called "the oriental philosophy," a Hermetic angelology that posited a middle reality between ordinary perceptions and the realm of the divine. This middle world of angelic perception is equated with the human world of the awakened imagination, the dwelling place of sages and poets, and of all of us in certain exalted or enlightened moments when we see, feel, and think most lucidly. Those moments, according to the Sufis, introduce us into what they call the world of Hurqalya, the angelic world. Hurqalya is called both a city and world, and sometimes is also named "the Celestial Earth," since it is our earth reimagined. Angelic imagination is a difficult mode of apprehension, and Sufism is primarily a discipline as well as a gnosis. Hurqalya has both a hell and a heaven, and is the city/country of the unexpected, where the past is not yet completed and so can be altered, and where the present and the future are always intermixed, so that resurrection is both here and to come. A study of the omens of Millennium is a proper place to invoke Hurqalya, since all of the omens are at home there, if we raise them into the mind, which is one of the functions of this book.

In the ninth century, the Islamic historian Tabari described a strange region, one that we would now think of as part of a story by Borges, a country of the imagination, the "Earth of the Emerald Cities." These cities (whose names have never been explained) are Jabarsa and Jabalqa and also Hurqalya, the name sometimes given to the visionary land as a whole. Corbin follows Tabari in a lucid description of these cities, which he joins the Sufis in regarding as quite real, realer indeed than Paris, London, and New York:

> Jabarsa and Jabalqa, Tabari tells us, are two emerald cities that lie immediately beyond the mountain of Qaf. Like those of the Heavenly Jerusalem, their dimensions express quaternity, the symbol of perfection and wholeness. The surface of each is a square, the sides measuring twelve thou-

sand parasangs. The inhabitants do not know of the existence of our Adam, nor of Iblis, the Antagonist; their food consists exclusively of vegetables; they have no need of clothing, for their faith in God makes them like the angels, although they are not angels. Since they are not differentiated by sex, they have no desire for posterity. Lastly, all their light comes to them from the mountain of Qaf, while the minerals in their soil and in the walls of their towns . . . secrete their own light.

Qaf is an emerald mountain surrounding our world; if you can climb beyond it, then you will see the visionary cities that represent what Corbin calls "the state of the Image" of the Resurrection Body. Perhaps influenced by Sufism, the Kabbalah names such an Image the *zelem,* the word used in Genesis when we are told that God created us in his own image. Hurqalya, sometimes also called by Sufis "the Eighth Climate" (seven being nature's) is the goal of the Gnostic quest to know the resurrection while still in this life.

Ibn 'Arabi, the foremost Sufi theosophist, created the major myth for understanding the mystical Earth of Hurqalya. After God had created Adam from the moistened red clay, a quantity of the clay was left over. God employs the clay both to make the palm tree, "the Sister of Adam," and the Earth of True Reality, Hurqalya, which contains for each of our souls a universe corresponding to that soul. Each soul has an Image in which it can contemplate itself, and so at last resurrect itself. Frequently the Image will be personified as Idris-Hermes, the Man of Light, or astral body, the figure of Perfect Nature of the guardian angel, one's alter ego. Shaikh Ahmad Ahsa'i suggestively adds: "The world of Hurqalya is a material world (the world of matter in the subtle state), which is *other*." To be material but *other* is a metaphor for the alter ego, for the weirdness of a guardian angel who is nevertheless one's own soul. We are carried back to the absolute strangeness of Genesis 1:26, where God said, "Let us make man in our image, after our likeness." Gershom Scholem, expounding the Kabbalistic concept of the *ʒelem,* Image or astral body, remarked that this "served the Kabbalists as a catchword for a notion bearing only a loose connection to the biblical idea." And yet God must have had something like an "image" or "likeness" of his own, as Scholem also said. God, however transcendent, is also someone who, in some sense, has the form of a man, an image in three dimensions, material yet an *other.* Though the origins of the astral body, as an image, are in Neoplatonism, it amalgamated rapidly with Judaic, Christian, and Islamic traditions. The Kabbalistic *ʒelem,* in particular, came to be regarded as the principle of individuation in each of us. It may seem a long path from the astral body to one's personal defining form, but the identity between the angelic being who guides one's "star" and the inner essence persists all through the mingled monotheistic traditions. The astral body, however esoteric it may seem, is finally the metaphor for what renders the self truly the self, rather than someone else's self.

In our current epidemic of "near-death experiences" the crucial image almost always is the person of Light who at last embraces the apparently departing self. My favorite among Henry Corbin's many remarkable books, *The Man of Light in*

Iranian Sufism, is the fullest exposition I know of this prevailing image of the Resurrection Body. Corbin quotes an account from Abul-Barakat of Baghdad, a Jewish sage who died about 1165, having converted to Islam at the age of ninety:

> This is why the ancient Sages, initiated into things the sensory faculties do not perceive, maintained that for each individual soul, or perhaps for several together having the same nature and affinity, there is a being in the spiritual world which throughout their existence watches over this soul and group of souls with especial solicitude and tenderness, leads them to knowledge, protects, guides, defends, comforts them, leads them to victory; and this being is what they call *Perfect Nature*. This friend, defender and protector is what in religious terminology is called the *Angel*.

The Perfect Nature is Hermes, the Angel Idris, or Enoch-Metatron. Scholem, commenting upon Abul-Barakat, catches the center of this doctrine: "Emptying the prophet of his everyday self permits him to absorb his angelic self." But what about those of us who are not prophets? We all of us, according to nearly every esoteric tradition, have an astral body. The Sufis indeed thought we had four astral bodies, and various other traditions assign us anywhere between two and five. Whether or not bodies two through five ever are *perceived* may depend upon one's status as a prophet, which is a recognition that brings the astral body and its companions closer to considerations of psychology than to those of occultism or esoteric philosophy.

Scholem says of the Kabbalistic *ʒelem* that it is each person's principle of individuation, so that in some sense it must be one's most authentic body, even if one encounters it only at the moment of one's death. Moshe Idel, Scholem's revisionary successor, rather surprisingly comes close to equating the *zelem* with the *golem,* the figure of the "artificial anthropoid" built by Rabbi Judah Loew of Prague. That would make the *golem,* like Dr. Frankenstein's *daemon,* or "monster," the double or "ghost" of the Kabbalistic Loew. Sometimes the Kabbalah refers to the astral body as the "shadow," so that Idel usefully warns us, however implicitly, that the *zelem,* or astral body, has a double potential: nightmare and Resurrection Body. This antithesis is too readily ignored in our current "near-death experiences," but it remains to be explored later in this book.

IMMORTALITY AND RESURRECTION

If the emphasis of this book was not almost exclusively upon Western tradition, then immortality, even in the shadows of the Millennium, would hardly be a disputable subject. Eastern traditions, particularly Indian, are very decisive upon what is, for many among us, a perplexity at best. Indian psychology, however divided in other matters, tends to insist that the inner self is indestructible. That inner self is also inactive: according to *The Bhagavad-Gita,* it does not kill, and cannot be killed. Yet it can *appear* active, because it is linked to the subtle, or astral, body (*linga*), which is not deferred until dying and death, as it tends to have been in our traditions. The subtle body acts, and can appear to kill or be killed, yet always it can return again. In the *Gita* the warrior Arjuna conducts an agonized dialogue with his charioteer Krishna, who is a kind of mortal god. Reluctant to go into battle against his kinsmen, friends, and teachers, Arjuna is persuaded by Krishna's counsel:

> He who thinks this self a killer
> and he who thinks it killed,
> both fail to understand;
> it does not kill, nor is it killed.
> It is not born,
> it does not die;
> having been,
> it will never not be;
> unborn, enduring,
> constant, and primordial,
> it is not killed
> when the body is killed.
>
> Arjuna, when a man knows the self
> to be indestructible, enduring, unborn,
> unchanging, how does he kill
> or cause anyone to kill?
> —translated by Barbara Stoler Miller

The individual self seems here to be compounded, by Krishna, with Brahman, the ultimate, universal self, but what the Western mind takes to be a confusion or an amalgam is no puzzle for Krishna, or for much of Hinduism. Death, for Hinduism, leads to the long, nearly endless process of transmigration, a wheel of existences. Western traditions have their analogues, if only because of Iranian influences upon early Judaism and later Islam, since the Iranians and Indians have a common origin. Norman Cohn's *Cosmos, Chaos and the World to Come* (1993), which I cited earlier, argues persuasively that Western religious visions of Millennium and resurrection stem from the Iranian prophet Zarathustra (better known by the Greek form of his name, Zoroaster). Certainly such visions do not emerge directly from the central works that make up the Hebrew Bible, which does not speak of the immortality of a soul or of a self until the prophets and psalmists of the Babylonian captivity sing their songs of Zion. There is only one apocalyptic book in the Hebrew Bible—Daniel—and it, like the Enoch apocalypses in the Apocrypha, clearly reflects Iranian influences. Indo-Iranian assumptions concerning an indestructible self simply were not Israelite phenomena. Pharisaic beliefs in the resurrection of the body took some of their basis from Ezekiel and the Second Isaiah, but more I suspect from Hellenistic influences. We have seen something of the Indo-Iranian intimations of immortality; Greek conceptions were rather different, and had a subtler effect upon Judaic views, and subsequently upon Christian and Islamic convictions. But these were later, Hellenistic views; Homeric and early Hebrew views are almost equally dark, and the differences between Hades and Sheol are hardly overwhelming. There is a remarkable, posthumously published study by the Virgilian scholar W. F. Jackson Knight, completed and edited for publication by his brother,

G. Wilson Knight, my favorite among all modern literary critics. Both Knights were convinced spiritualists, and their peculiar faith contaminates *Elysion: On Ancient Greek and Roman Beliefs Concerning a Life After Death* (1970). And yet the book remains remarkably illuminating, particularly from the Hellenistic period onwards, in its evidence of the classical tradition's tendency to maintain a virtually incessant communication with the dead. At the least, the Knights performed the service of returning us to the great book by E. R. Dodds, *The Greeks and the Irrational* (1951), in which the doctrine of rebirth is seen as the shamanistic element in Greek religion. The *daemon,* magical or occult self, is distinguished from the *psyche,* or soul, and it is the *daemon* which survives to endure a sequence of rebirths.

What is the link between immortality and Millennium? Or to rephrase, in terms of the central argument of this book: why is "not dying" one of the prime omens of the coming Millennium? Norman Cohn assigns to Zoroaster the ultimate responsibility for creating the millennarian consciousness, which would be with us now even if the end of the twentieth century were not nearly so imminent. America, as I will show in my final chapter, is inevitably the most millennarian of all nations, even though so far it has avoided the two extremes of modern millennarianism, fascism and Marxist-Leninism. But all Western angelology seems to me, ultimately, to owe more to Zoroaster than to any other religious genius.

The fundamental imagining of Zoroaster is a separation of all reality into two forces, the sublime Light of Ormazd, or God, and the abyss of Darkness associated with Ahriman, Death, or the Devil. (The Devil, though he is a composite of several traditions, owes almost nothing to the Hebrew Bible, and almost as much to Zoroaster as Shelley suggested he does to John Milton.) We dwell in a mixed condition, between Light and Darkness, but this cosmic dualism is not the crucial aspect of Zoroastrianism, even though that is the popular view. Each of us, according to Zoroaster, has what is now called a guardian angel, a celestial being of Light who is our prototype. Our confrontation with the angel is neither empirical nor transcendental; instead it takes place in a middle world that Henry Corbin calls "imaginal," which is neither imaginary nor what generally we call "imaginative," in the Western aesthetic sense. For the Zoroastrians, as for their Iranian descendants, the Shi'ite Sufis, or Gnostics, the imaginal world, Hurqalya, or "Earth of Resurrection," is where resurrection takes place. It features what Corbin calls "a physics and physiology of Resurrection," which I will expound later in this chapter. What Corbin does not bother to say seems to me to require greater emphasis, as we drift on towards Millennium: it is this imaginal or middle world, and not the suprasensible realm of God, that provides our intimations of immortality and that holds the promise of resurrection. There is indeed no pragmatic difference between the ideas of immortality and of resurrection in Zoroastrianism or in Iranian Islam. So large a dislocation exists between this vision and our customary modes of expectation and faith as regards what we want to call an "afterlife" that this contrast needs consideration if I am to go further in this account of what could be termed the Gnosis of the world to come. I am aware of the irony that politically Iran is now the West's most implacable enemy, so that religious understanding of its spiritual legacy may yet have some pragmatic importance.

There is a perpetual ambiguity in the relation between two ideas that we tend to identify in a Christian or post-Christian society: immortality and resurrection. This ambiguity returns us to a central ambivalence both in Western history and in Christian theology: our thought-forms are Greek, our morality and faith ultimately are Hebraic, and much in the ancient Greek and Hebrew visions was profoundly antithetical to one another. The immortality of the soul, as we generally apprehend it, is a Platonic notion: its heroic exemplar is Socrates. Resurrection seems to have begun as a Zoroastrian idea, but its crucial development came with the intertestamental Jews, and its great exemplar is Jesus. The Socratic soul requires no resurrection, because it cannot die. Jesus, like the Pharisees, believes that his soul must stand before God for judgment, and again, like the Pharisees, Jesus believes that his body will be resurrected. Though Greek immortality and Jewish Christian resurrection have been and still are being richly confused, they do not appear to me as compatible beliefs. I follow here the Swiss theologian Oscar Cullmann, who, in a celebrated Harvard lecture of 1955, rigorously distinguished between the Socratic and primitive Christian ideas.

Cullmann reminds us that in the New Testament we are told that death is "the last enemy," whereas Socrates greets death as a friend. For the early Christians, Cullmann adds, "The soul is not intrinsically immortal" but became so only through the resurrection of Jesus Christ, and through faith in that resurrection. Finally, Cullmann insists, the full resurrection will come, but only when on "the last day" the body is forever resurrected. Yet in the meantime, death is the enemy of God, for Jesus, but not for Socrates, and so Jesus and Socrates confront death very differently indeed. Saint Paul, like the Hellenistic Jews, seems to have absorbed Platonic notions of immortality, but there seems no Platonic influence upon Jesus himself, with his altogether Pharisaic belief in resurrection: "He is not God of the dead but of the living." The intertestamental Jewish texts that fuse immortality and resurrection are themselves Platonized, but Jesus, despite the New Testament polemic against the Pharisees falsely argued in his name, seems less Platonized even than the Pharisees. He is in the tradition of "Yahweh alone," even if his vision of Yahweh is extraordinarily benign, at least in those passages of the Gospels (and *The Gospel of Thomas*) that have the authentic aura of his voice.

Why did the Jews, for rather more than a thousand years before the Pharisees, have no doctrine either of immortality or of resurrection? The Yahwist, or J Writer, the original and most powerful (in the literary and cognitive senses) of Hebrew writers, takes individual death as a finality. Like Homer, the biblical authors see the after-death existence as a mere flickering of shades, whether in Homer's Hades or the Hebraic Sheol. Still, there was Enoch, who did not die but was taken away by Yahweh, and Elijah, who also ascended, without the necessity of dying. Post-Exilic Judaism could rely upon Ezekiel's vision of the dry bones living again, and one suspects a Zoroastrian stimulus as operant upon Ezekiel in the Exile. By time of Judas Maccabeus, in the Jewish struggle against the Hellenistic Syrians, the idea of resurrection was in dispute among Jews, and 2 Maccabees clearly indicates that the Maccabeans held for the resurrection. How lively a concern this was is unclear to me; Jesus himself (except in Gnostic texts) does not tell us much about resurrection. The Jewish Christians of Jerusalem, Saint Paul's opponents, may have had much in common with the Gnostic Christians a century later, and so may have viewed the Resurrection more as an inward than as a Pauline historical event. As I have already mentioned, it is one of the many extraordinary puzzles of the canonical New Testament that it tells us almost nothing of what Jesus said and did when he tarried with his disciples in the interval between Resurrection and Ascension. Gnosticism, like the American Gnosis of Mormonism, has something to say of this interval, but it was evidently of little interest to Paul and to those who came after him. I wonder always how the early Christians could have failed to preserve the actual Aramaic text of Jesus' own sayings, a wonder akin to my bafflement as to the Pauline lack of curiosity concerning the words and activities of the risen Christ.

The early Christian theologian Origen remarked that Christ appeared not only in his common guise and in transfigured form, but also "to every man according as the man merited." Origen provides an entry to the most complex question that attends the Resurrection of Jesus: did he return as phantasm or as the institutional dogma of Christianity, a Resurrection Incarnation that fuses flesh and image? The Gnostic view, adopted by the Koran, is that the Resurrection was "Docetic," that is, apparitional and subjective, seen according to the spiritual merit of the observer. Henry Corbin argues that the manifestation of the resurrected Jesus depends upon each individual soul's aptitude for seeing a divine figure: "The dominant intuition is that the soul is not the witness of an external event but the medium *in which* the event takes place." As Corbin says, Docetism is not a doctrine (like the Incarnation) but a tendency, one that "can conceive of the reality of a body intermediate between the sensible and the intelligible." This Gnostic Christ has been called, in ancient times, "the Angel Christ," appearing as a man to men, as an angel to angels, according to Origen. Such a Christ excludes nearly any possibility of dogma: Christ's virgin birth can be accepted, or rejected, Corbin notes, because the distinction between literal and symbolic has vanished. Christian dogma is Pauline and post-Pauline; the Jesus of the proto-Gnostic *Gospel of Thomas* cannot be reconciled with any dogma, and I have never understood why Christian scholars almost invariably incline to Paul, rather than to the Church of Jerusalem, headed by James the Just, brother of Jesus and clear inheritor of his legacy. Scholars, themselves dogmatists, seem to worship the winning side in history, and Paul won.

Islam, in its origins, partly represented a return to the faith of the Ebionites, the descendants of the Jewish Christians led by James the Just. A few scholars, particularly Oscar Cullmann and H. J. Schoeps, have demonstrated that the first church at Jerusalem, as close to an authentic primitive Christianity as we can come, had no use for the Pauline dogma of the Incarnation, in which Jesus is at once God and man, and so constitutes a second Adam replacing the fallen first Adam. Against this the Jewish Christians, and many Christian Gnostics and Moslem mystics after them, held to the vision that Adam was a true, un-

fallen prophet, indeed higher than the angels, and thus incapable of sin. Somewhere behind this, and now untraceable,
there was an earlier Jewish Gnosis, perhaps largely an oral tradition, that was to flourish more than a thousand years later in
medieval Provençal and Spanish Kabbalah. This ultimate vision
of Adam, preserved later in Hermetic and Christian heterodox
texts, has been called the doctrine of the God-Man, the
primeval Anthropos. Sometimes this God-Adam was seen as
identical with the highest God himself, so that the earthly Adam
appeared as a copy or reflection of this original. But other times,
God makes a "Son of Man," which is the copy, and this Son of
Man becomes the paradigm of a third Adam, the protagonist of
Genesis. Again, in some versions of the myth, the second Adam
falls (or is enticed) into the third, and so becomes the *pneuma*,
"spirit," "spark," or "inner man," that Gnostics always identify
as the deep self.

The Gnostic Jesus therefore requires no descent from King
David, and needs no Mary as mother. In one Jewish Christian
Gospel, Jesus speaks of the Holy Spirit as his mother, who
seized him by the hair and ascended with him up to Mount Ta-
bor. Only the Angel Christ is pre-existent, and he is the figure
captured by the Holy Spirit. There is thus no Passion, only an
Illumination that is a knowing of the truth. We are very close to
the Jesus of the Koran, one all but identified with the angel
Gabriel, who gave Muhammad his revelation. Gabriel, Jesus,
and Adam all are forms of Christos ("the anointed one"), and
all represent the Holy Spirit of prophecy. It is in this matrix that
the distinction between Greek "immortality" and Hebrew-
Christian "resurrection" truly loses all persuasiveness. The

Adam of the Anthropos myth *is* immortality, and our return to him, and his to us, is the Resurrection. The Resurrection of the body is the restoration of Adam.

THE RESURRECTION BODY

In the eloquent epilogue to his *The Body and Society: Men, Women, and Sexual Renunciation in Early Christianity* (1988), the historian Peter Brown summed up the connections between asceticism and the hope of resurrection in the late fifth and the sixth centuries:

> The human body was poised on the threshold of a mighty change. In Christian circles, concern with sexual renuncia-tion had never been limited solely to an anxious striving to maximize control over the body. It had been connected with a heroic and sustained attempt, on the part of thinkers of widely different background and temper of mind, to map out the horizons of human freedom. The light of a great hope of future transformation glowed behind even the most austere statements of the ascetic position. To many, conti-nence had declared the end of the tyranny of the "present age." In the words of John Chrysostom, virginity made plain that "the things of the resurrection stand at the door."

Behind this Christian view of resurrection, as Brown demonstrates, is the ferocious question of Saint Paul: "Who will deliver me from this body of death?" This is the dogmatic

Christian formulation which, to the Christian Gnostics, and to the Jewish Christians of James's Church before them, turned the Resurrection of Jesus inside out. The Valentinian Gnostic *Gospel of Philip* replied, "While we are still in the world it is fitting for us to acquire this resurrection for ourselves." A still subtler reply was made by Origen of Alexandria, in the third century, for Origen was neither a dogmatic Incarnationist nor a Gnostic:

> Origen bequeathed to his successors a view of the human person that continued to inspire, to fascinate, and to dismay all later generations. He conveyed, above all, a profound sense of the fluidity of the body. Basic aspects of human beings, such as sexuality, sexual differences, and other seemingly indestructible attributes of the person associated with the physical body, struck Origen as no more than provisional. The present human body reflected the needs of a single, somewhat cramped moment in the spirit's progress back to a former, limitless identity (Brown, p. 167).

So fluid a view of the body was consonant with Origen's idea, cited earlier, that the resurrected Jesus appeared as a man to men and as an angel to angels. Origen, desiring to preserve an identity between our natural and our resurrected bodies, followed the remark of Jesus in Luke 20:36, that in the resurrection we are "equal unto angels." As in Plato, both bodies have an element of "ether," or air, but the resurrected ones are more ethereal, subtler, yet retaining "the characteristic form" of our animal bodies. Literal identity between the two bodies, which was the dogmatic insistence of most fathers of the Church, is dismissed by Origen, who sees resurrection as the union of the soul and a purified identity. An inner form, like a grain of wheat, is sown in our bodies, and out of this the Resurrection Body will rise, perhaps not looking at all the way we used to look. The kindly and shrewd Origen thus avoided the peculiar question Tertullian had asked: "What will be the use of the entire body, when the entire body shall become useless?" Like the other fathers, Tertullian had no answer, except to say that in the presence of God there would be no idleness!

The contrast between Origen and Tertullian can serve as prelude to a discussion of the difficulties involved in all speculations upon our bodies in a general resurrection. Caroline Walker Bynum, in *The Resurrection of the Body in Western Christianity, 200–1336* (1995), outlines the Patristic debates that went on from the age of Tertullian (around 200) through the era of Origen and Augustine (around 400). Her interpretive insight establishes many of the ongoing continuities between "seed images" in the Church fathers and the curious proliferation of similar images in our current popular culture. For Christian tradition, the image begins with Paul in 1 Corinthians 15, where a natural body is sown, but rises as a spiritual body. What *is* a spiritual body? Bynum's study resolutely seeks a materialist answer, just as Henry Corbin, on behalf of his Shi'ite Sufis, quests for an imaginal realm midway between material and spiritual. A purely spiritual answer does not seem to suit our age, when so many of the demarcations between the material and the imaginal tend to vanish, as our "science" turns more self-reflexive. In the context of medieval materialist images of resurrection, Bynum rather wonderfully asks: "Why is the reconstitution of my toe or fingernail a reward for virtue?" She asks that in the spirit of Origen, and also of Thomas Aquinas a thousand years after Origen, both of whom sought a nonmaterial solution to the problem of preserved identity in resurrection.

Origen's view remains condemned by the Church, and even Aquinas was condemned, in this regard, though vindicated by the Church a generation later. Yet the major Catholic emphasis, to this day, remains materialist, though only in the pure good of dogma, as it were. Contemporary Catholics and mainline Protestants alike say they believe in resurrection, yet they generally mean a survival that involves some wraithlike entity. American religionists of our indigenous varieties more frequently return to the older belief in the resurrection of the body, and many among them indeed, like the ancient Gnostics, already have experienced resurrection in this life. I have argued elsewhere (in *The American Religion*, 1992) that there is a pervasive American *knowing*, almost of Gnosis in the ancient sense, that one's deepest self is no part of the Creation, but is as old as God, being a spark or particle of God. Americans truly believe that God loves them, and they frequently interpret this as meaning that they have walked with Jesus, the Jesus who went about with his disciples in a forty-day interval between his Resurrection and his Ascension. I return here to my point that the New Testament and Christian dogma after it tell us almost nothing about those forty days:

> To whom also he showed himself alive after his passion
> by many infallible proofs, being seen of them forty days, and
> speaking of the things pertaining to the Kingdom of God.
> —The Acts of the Apostles 1:3

What were, what are those things pertaining to the Kingdom of God? Where dogmatic Christianity has been silent or evasive, heterodox tradition has known, or at the least speculated. Apocryphal and Gnostic texts attained their apotheosis in an extraordinary proto-Gnostic "hidden sayings of Jesus," *The Gospel of Thomas*, which promises resurrection through an act of understanding: "whoever discovers the interpretation of these sayings will not taste death." Composed presumably towards the end of the first century, possibly in Syria, *The Gospel of Thomas* may well include authentic sayings of Jesus not available elsewhere. There is no dogma in *The Gospel of Thomas:* Jesus is a wisdom teacher, who will not be crucified and then ascend. He will require no resurrection, because he proclaims that resurrection is all around us. Since he gives highest praise to his brother, James the Just, head of the Jewish Christian Church, I assume that this may have been a text of that group, but later revised and very likely censored by a Syrian ascetic monk. But in spirit, *The Gospel of Thomas* inhabits that interval of forty days spoken of in Acts, an interval already indefinitely extended in the hidden sayings of Jesus, and almost infinitely extended by American religionists, who see the interval as a timeless present.

One way of seeing just how radical *The Gospel of Thomas* truly becomes in a Western world still overtly professing institutional and historical Christianity is to contrast it to Saint Augustine's interpretation of Saint Paul's "spiritual body." In *The City of God*, Augustine says that this spiritual body is one's own body but only when "subject to the spirit, readily offering total and wonderful obedience." In *The Gospel of Thomas:*

Jesus said, "I am not your teacher. Because you have drunk, you have become intoxicated from the bubbling spring that I have tended."

—translated by Marvin Meyer

Intoxication is rather different from obedience; you can be obedient either in the physical or the spiritual world, but not in the extended interval of resurrection, which is an imaginal world in the rather rigorous sense derived by Henry Corbin from his Sufi precursors. When Enoch walked with God, and he was not, because God took him, we are in that middle world, the realm of the Resurrection Body, of the angels of prophetic dreams, of walking with Jesus, of Gnosis throughout the ages. As Corbin says, this mediating power of the imaginal is a cognitive force in its own right, though unrecognized by most modes of philosophy. We are in an intermediate realm between pure matter and pure spirit. Empiricists and supernaturalists alike may dismiss this middle sphere as a fiction, but imaginative men and women, whether literary in their orientation or not, will recognize that the imaginal world exists, and is not fantasy or wish fulfillment. I set aside the question of prayer when I make these remarks, which are neither Gnostic nor agnostic in their design. The imagination of the Resurrection Body need be neither a prayer nor a poem nor a desperate lunge at a materialist revivification; it need not be myth nor metaphor nor part of a Jungian cult of a divinized unconscious. To cite a very different tradition than that of Corbin's Sufis, I turn to the great Talmudist Adin Steinsaltz's *The Thirteen Petalled Rose* (translated by Yehuda Hanegbi, 1980). The title refers to the opening passage of the *Zohar,* itself a commentary upon the Song of Songs: "As the rose among the thorns, so is my love among the maidens" (2:2). Avoiding most of the technical vocabulary of the Kabbalah, Steinsaltz begins with a chapter upon the four "Worlds" according to Kabbalah: "emanation," "creation," "formation," and "action," from higher to lower. "Action" is the empirical realm, while "formation" is the imaginal world, where Kabbalah and Steinsaltz locate the angels. Without going into the vexed problem of how Jewish, Aristotelian, Neoplatonic, and possibly even Indian and Iranian sources fuse together, both in Sufism and Kabbalah, one can observe that Steinsaltz faithfully follows the Zoharic scheme. The world of emanation belongs to the ten *sefirot,* the basic building blocks of Kabbalah, while the world of creation centers upon the Throne and Chariot (*Merkabah*) of God. The world of formation centers upon Metatron, once Enoch, the prince of the angels, while the world of action or making is that of ordinary perception. Steinsaltz charmingly emphasizes, as does Corbin in his account of the Sufi imaginal world, that our perception of angels can be quite as ordinary as if such messengers dwelt entirely in the world of action:

> The creation of an angel in our world and the immediate relegation of this angel to another world is, in itself, not at all a supernatural phenomenon; it is a part of a familiar realm of experience, an integral piece of life, which may even seem ordinary and commonplace because of its traditional rootedness in the system of *mitzvot* [good deeds], or the order of sanctity. When we are in the act of creating the

angel, we have no perception of the angel being created, and this act seems to be a part of the whole structure of the practical material world in which we live. Similarly, the angel who is sent to us from another world does not always have a significance or impact beyond the normal laws of physical nature. Indeed, it often happens that the angel precisely reveals itself in nature, in the ordinary common-sense world of causality, and only a prophetic insight or divination can show when, and to what extent, it is the work of higher forces. For man by his very nature is bound to the system of higher worlds, even though ordinarily this system is not revealed and known to him. As a result, the system of higher worlds seems to him to be natural, just as the whole of his two-sided existence, including both matter and spirit, seems self-evident to him. Man does not wonder at all about those passages he goes through all the time in the world of action, from the realm of material existence to the realm of spiritual existence. What is more, the rest of the other worlds that also penetrate our world may appear to us as part of something quite natural. It may be said that the realities of the angel and of the world of formation are part of a system of "natural" being which is as bound by law as that aspect of existence we are able to observe directly. Therefore neither the existence of the angel nor his "mission," taking him from world to world, need break through the reality of nature in the broadest sense of the word. (Steinsaltz, pp. 15–16).

That "prophetic insight or divination" is the imaginal at work interpreting what essentially is our common (and commonplace) existence. What happens when such insight or divination interprets our bodies? Corbin's Sufi sages contented themselves with just three worlds, by compounding the two higher realms that Kabbalists called emanation and creation into a single domain of pure Intelligences. That left the middle kingdom of the imaginal, place of angels and of souls, and the lower, sensible world of material objects. Love, in every sense that is not just what Freud named as the sexual drive, clearly inhabits the world of formation or the imaginal. Corbin says that "One does not penetrate into the Angelic World by housebreaking," a remark equally applicable to the domain of love. Love, interpreting the body of the other, participates in a divination or insight that should be called "prophetic." What Sufism (and Christian Gnosticism before it) terms the Resurrection Body is what many of us encounter, in some rare moments of our lives, as the body of love. There have been remarkable evocations of that body in the greatest poets, Dante and Shakespeare in particular, but for a more systematic account I follow Henry Corbin in relying upon Shaikh Ahmad Ahsa'i, the Iranian Shi'ite founder of the Shaikhi school of Sufism. The Shaikh, who died in 1826, expounded a doctrine with elements of Hermetism, Neoplatonism, and Gnosticism fused into what Corbin calls "something like a physics of Resurrection and a physiology of the 'body of resurrection.'" Even without going into his technicalities (and esoteric Iranian terms), the Shaikh's imaginal portrait of the Resurrection Body retains a cogency and coherence sadly absent from our current New Age equivalents.

Each human being, Corbin comments, possesses four aspects of a body. Corbin charts them, and I adapt them here in simplified form:

1. The "elemental" or apparent body, the one that we can see, touch, and weigh: it is accidental and perishable. Let us call it the "apparent body," for convenience.

2. Within (1) there is a hidden body, also elemental but essential and imperishable: "spiritual flesh," as Corbin calls it, which I will adopt.

3. The traditional "astral body," not elemental yet still accidental, not everlasting, because it will be reabsorbed by divinity in the resurrection. I will call it the "astral body" proper.

4. The eternal, subtle body, essential and angelic, the ultimate guarantee of individuality, and akin to the *ẓelem* of Kabbalah and the "immortal body" of the Hermetic writings. Let us call it the "angelic body."

What are the advantages, spiritual and expositional, of this fourfold scheme? Its added complexity is to give us two versions of the astral body of tradition, "astral" yet not eternal, and "angelic" or everlasting. The relation between the "apparent body" and "spiritual flesh" is parallel to that between the "astral body" and the "angelic body." Since orthodox, Sunni Islam interpreted the Koran as literally as many Christians have read the New Testament, resurrection to them meant the return to the "apparent body," just as it was. But in the Shi'ite Sufi vision, both the "apparent body" and the "astral body" eventually vanish, while a fusion of "spiritual flesh" and "angelic body" ultimately abides. That "spiritual flesh" is equivalent to the ancient Gnostic metaphor of the "spark," or innermost self, which is no part of Creation but is already a particle of God, since it is as old as God. When Gnostics, ancient or modern, speak of the Resurrection as already having taken place, they mean that they firmly distinguish between the outward body and the spark. The Sufi "angelic body" is akin to the ancient Gnostic "Angel Christ," the fulfilled form of the surviving sparks. But there still remains the subtle imaginal distinction between the "astral" and "angelic" bodies. What can we gain by resorting to this distinction?

Essentially, the Shaikhis' complexity renews the ancient Gnostic difference between soul (or *psyche*), and self (or *pneuma*, or spark). The "astral body" is like the Gnostic soul, and both are impermanent. The spark, or "spiritual flesh," survives and rejoins a more authentic soul, in a fusion of self and angelic soul that truly is the Resurrection Body, and that guarantees a survival of individual identity, while dispensing with the accidental "apparent body" and accidental soul, or "astral body." Whatever new difficulties are involved in this conception of the Resurrection Body, we have gained an imaginal understanding of the spiritual conviction and knowledge that one can experience what it is to be "spiritual flesh" in this life. To expound that understanding, I turn now to a chapter on Gnosis itself, in four of its major historical embodiments: Hermetism, Christian Gnosticism, Sufism, and the Kabbalah.

CHAPTER 4

GNOSIS

The Hermetic Corpus: Divine Man

Earlier in this book I discussed the fused identity of five figures: Seth, the son of Adam, the Hebrew patriarch Enoch, the angel Metatron, the Greco-Egyptian god Hermes, and the Muslim angel Idris. Hermeticism was neither the first gnosis nor the first Gnosticism, but it always has operated as the spirit of fusion between different esoteric traditions. In many ways our current millenarian preoccupations—with angels, telepathic dreams, "out-of-the-body" and "near-death experiences"—can be called an American Hermeticism. Scholars call the original, Greco-Egyptian doctrine of Hermes by the name "Hermetism," so as to distinguish it from its Renaissance and modern descendants, and I will follow that example here.

Hermetism appears to have been a pagan religious movement, probably quite small, in Hellenistic Alexandria of the first century of our Common Era. The best study of it is *The Egyptian Hermes* by Garth Fowden (1986), and there is a superb translation of the surviving texts, Brian P. Copenhaver's *Hermetica* (1992). Together, Fowden and Copenhaver have done for Hermetism what Gershom Scholem did and Moshe Idel goes on doing for Kabbalism, and what Henry Corbin did for Shi'ite Sufism: each of these established the foundation for all future study. Gnosticism, a more complex and bewildering phenomenon than any of these, has had a score of distinguished scholars, among whom Hans Jonas was particularly outstanding. Hermetism, though it probably began as an affair of only a handful or two of Alexandrian pagan intellectuals, probably has been the most influential of all these traditions, because of what can only be called celebrated errors about its dating and its nature.

Anyone who has been inside the extraordinary cathedral in Siena, Italy, is likely to remember the remarkable picture of Hermes Mercurius Trismegistus as rendered by Giovanni di Stefano in 1488. This *Thrice Greatest Hermes* took his place in a Catholic cathedral because in 1462 Cosimo de' Medici, of the great Florentine governing house, commissioned the humanist Marsilio Ficino to translate the *Hermetica* from Greek into Latin. Cosimo and Ficino, and their contemporaries, believed that the Hermetic writings had been composed in Egypt about the time that Moses was born, so that these texts therefore were older than the Five Books of Moses, and actually were held to constitute the "ancient theology." The supposed author, Hermes, was believed to have prophesied the birth and ruin of Judaism, the coming of Christ, and the Last Judgment and General Resurrection. It was not until 1614 that the scholar Isaac Casaubon demonstrated that the *Hermetica* were not works preceding Moses. The later fifteenth century and all of the sixteenth were permeated by a Hermetic fervor that reached apocalyptic pitch in the great magus Giordano Bruno, martyred by the Church for his replacement of Christ by Hermes. Long after the exposures by Casaubon had been accepted, Hermeticism remained the basis for European alchemy and occultism.

The original Hermetism seems to me more vital than its Renaissance descendant, and in some ways is very much with us still. The Light or person of Light who embraces our current survivors of the "near-death experience" is the Egyptian Hermes himself, the psychopomp who leads us to the land of the dead. There remains much of value to be learned by carefully reading the *Hermetica,* tractates actually composed in Hellenistic Egypt towards the end of the first century of the Common Era, which is when the Gospel of John, most belated of the Gospels, was written. Though pagan Platonists, the first Hermetists were much affected by Hellenistic Judaism and its allegorizings of the Bible, and the Gnosis at the heart of the *Hermetica* reminds us again that Gnosticism was a Jewish heresy before it became a Christian one. Jewish myths of a first or primordial Adam, Anthropos, or Man, inform the center of Hermetism, as at the close of *Hermetica X,* the discourse of Hermes Trismegistus called "The Key":

For the human is a godlike living thing, not comparable to the other living things of the earth but to those in heaven above, who are called gods. Or better—if one dare tell the truth—the one who is really human is above these gods as well, or at least they are wholly equal in power to one another.

For none of the heavenly gods will go down to earth, leaving behind the bounds of heaven, yet the human rises up to heaven and takes its measure and knows what is in its heights and its depths, and he understands all else exactly and—greater than all of this—he comes to be on high without leaving earth behind, so enormous is his range. Therefore, we must dare to say that the human on earth is a mortal god but that god in heaven is an immortal human. Through these two, then, cosmos and human, all things exist, but they all exist by action of the one.

—translated by Brian P. Copenhaver

Garth Fowden comments on how different this Hermetic way to divinization was from a mere rite of passage into death, thus joining oneself to a plurality of gods. Like the divine man of the Neoplatonist Plotinus, the Hermetist is assimilated to God himself, yet then "must descend from intellect to reasoning," after having been God. The Hermetist differs from the Neoplatonists because, like the Jew and the Christian, the Hermetist *knows* God. The nature of that knowledge allies Hermetism to both Jewish and Christian Gnosticism, as *experiential* modes of religion whose entire purpose is to abolish ignorance in order to learn the true nature of the origin. In the famous first discourse of the *Hermetica,* the *Poimandres,* the origin is one that fuses Creation and Fall in the authentic Gnostic pattern:

> Mind, the father of all, who is life and light, gave birth to a man like himself whom he loved as his own child. The man was most fair: he had the father's image; and god, who was really in love with his own form, bestowed on him all his craftworks. And after the man had observed what the craftsman had created with the father's help, he also wished to make some craftwork, and the father agreed to this. Entering the craftsman's sphere, where he was to have all authority, the man observed his brother's craftworks; the governors loved the man, and each gave a share of his own order. Learning well their essence and sharing in their nature, the man wished to break through the circumference of the circles to observe the rule of the one given power over the fire.
>
> Having all authority over the cosmos of mortals and unreasoning animals, the man broke through the vault and stooped to look through the cosmic framework, thus displaying to lower nature the fair form of god. Nature smiled for love when she saw him whose fairness brings no surfeit (and) who holds in himself all the energy of the governors and the form of god, for in the water she saw the shape of the man's fairest form and upon the earth its shadow. When the man saw in the water the form like himself as it was in nature, he loved it and wished to inhabit it; wish and action came in the same moment, and he inhabited the unreasoning form. Nature took hold of her beloved, hugged him all about and embraced him, for they were lovers.
>
> Because of this, unlike any other living thing on earth,

mankind is twofold—in the body mortal but immortal in the essential man. Even though he is immortal and has authority over all things, mankind is affected by mortality because he is subject to fate; thus, although man is above the cosmic framework, he became a slave within it. He is androgyne because he comes from an androgyne father, and he never sleeps because he comes from one who is sleepless. Yet love and sleep are his masters.

—translated by Brian P. Copenhaver

This is a Gnostic version of the Judaic Genesis, but not a violent revision or negation of it, like those to be found in Christian Gnosticism of the second century C.E. The Hermetist visionary laments our Fall into "love and sleep," in which the cosmos gains mastery over us, but we are culpable through our own narcissism, while "Mind, the father of all," is implicitly absolved of blame. And yet, what is the process that is so strikingly represented here? We are given the central story of all Gnosticism, the Fall of Anthropos the Primal Man or Adam-God, into the shape of the lower Adam, ourselves. Schooled as we are by Jewish and Christian accounts of this event, or by the angry Gnostic inversions of those accounts, we are likely at first to be lulled by the equable tone of this Hermetist version. Its affect is subtle and nostalgic, and also preternaturally quiet, even though it describes catastrophe rather than a fortunate Fall. To be drugged by the embrace of nature into what we call most natural in us, our sleepiness and our sexual desires, is at once a pleasant and an unhappy fate, since what remains immortal in us is both androgynous and sleepless.

The Pagan Gnosticism of the Hermetists is far gentler and more resigned concerning this paradox than anything to be encountered in Jewish or Christian Gnosticism. It will take certain Sufi sages, as we will see, to recover the poignance of the Hermetic double stance in regard to the fall of Divine Man. The Sufi Man of Light, a restored Hermes, is very close to the millennial image that haunts America in the final years of our century. Spiritual rebirth in the American Religion, in whatever ostensible denomination, is far closer to the patterns of Hermetism than to doctrinal, European Christianity. Emerson's "Self-Reliance" remains the American mode of self-knowledge, and is essentially Hermetic, not Christian. Initiation in American spiritual rebirth commences a process in which we become "healed, original, and pure," in the language of Hart Crane's "Passage," in which we are promised "an improved infancy." Fowden, expounding Hermetism, is perfectly appropriate to American evangelical accounts of the Second Birth: "Rebirth is emphatically not a repetition of physical birth, but a bursting into a new plane of existence previously unattained, even unsuspected, albeit available potentially."

CHRISTIAN GNOSTICISM:
VALENTINUS AND RESURRECTION

Many different meanings may be involved when most of us affirm: "I believe in God" or "I believe that Jesus Christ was and is the Son of God" or "There is no god but Allah, and Muham-

mad was the seal of the prophets" or "I trust in the Covenant."
Belief that something was, is, and will be so is generally what
we call faith, the mode of Western religion, in its principal currents, which can be traced back to the figure of Abraham, since
Judaism, Christianity, and Islam all are "children of Abraham."
Faith is a mode very different from knowledge, ambiguous as
knowledge may be in the religious sphere. If faith asserts that it
is knowledge, such an assertion remains different from a knowing that opposes itself to belief, in the inner conviction that
knowing is a more authentic way to God. When the knowing
represents itself as mutual, in which God knows the deep self
even as it knows God, then we have abandoned belief for Gnosis. This book essentially is about Gnosis, whether esoteric or
popular, whether ancient or modern. In a secondary sense only,
it also concerns Gnosticism, a heretical tradition that arose
within the earliest eras of Hebrew religion, and that was transmitted to aspects of Christianity and of Islam. There was (and
is) something that can be called, in Hans Jonas's phrase, "the
Gnostic religion," which depends upon Gnosis, but Gnosis
need not lead to any specific Gnosticism.

Since the various faiths of the children of Abraham continue to maintain their institutional status, Gnosis and Gnosticism frequently are deprecated, whether by normative scholars
or by neoconservative journalists. Historically, Western normative religion has much to expiate that was inhumane; the Gnostic religion, never in power, is free of that guilt. Gnosticism and
Gnosis once were elitist phenomena: religion for a relative few,
more often than not intellectuals. I do not see that this is to be
deplored, or extolled: spiritual imagination is hardly a universal

endowment. Blake, who had his own Gnosis, opined that one law for the lion and the ox was oppression, adding the defiance that what could be made explicit to the idiot was not worth his care. How explicit Gnosis can be made is a considerable puzzle to me, but that is part of the challenge I attempt to take on in this book. How does one explain Gnosis to those who very possibly have experienced it, yet did not know that they know, or what it was that was known, by them or of them? Once an elitist phenomenon, Gnosis has been domesticated in America for two centuries now, so that we have the paradox of a Gnostic nation that does not know it knows.

The experience of Gnosis is a varied phenomenon: your knowing may be prompted by a moment of utter solitude, or by the presence of another person. You may be reading or writing, watching an image or a tree, or gazing only inward. Gnosis, though related both to mysticism and to wisdom, is quite distinct from either. Mysticism, though it comes in many kinds, by no means opposes itself to faith; perhaps indeed it is the most intense form of faith. Wisdom, in the biblical sense, is allied with the prophetic reception of a God who dominates our world, which is seen as having fallen away from his original Creation. Gnosis grants you acquaintance with a God unknown to, and remote from, this world, a God in exile from a false creation that, in itself, constituted a fall. You yourself, in knowing and being known by this alienated God, come to see that originally your deepest self was no part of the Creation-Fall, but goes back to an archaic time before time, when that deepest self was part of a fullness that was God, a more human God than any worshipped since.

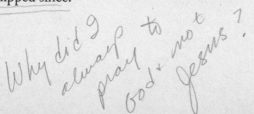

I am very aware that my last sentence requires much un-
packing, but it was designed for that purpose, because Gnosis is
entirely the doctrine of the deep or deepest self. Gnosis essentially is the act of distinguishing the *psyche*, or soul, from the
deep self, an act of distinction that is also a recognition. You
cannot strengthen your *psyche* without reacquainting yourself
with your original self, compared to which your *psyche* is only a
remnant, a wounded survivor. Peter Brown, in *The Body and
Society* (1988), his study of "Men, Women, and Sexual Renunciation in Early Christianity," expresses this succinctly, in an
analysis of the Gnostic doctrine of Valentinus:

> Even the soul, the *psychè*, the conscious self, had occurred as
> an afterthought. It swathed the lucid spirit in a thick fog of
> doubt, anxiety, and passion. The unredeemed lived as in a
> waking nightmare. All human thought, even the most pro-
> found religious quest, was riven with uncertainty and mis-
> placed ambition. Only the spirit had a right to exist. It stirred
> in the depths of the initiate with a blind, insistent "ferment,"
> which betrayed its distant origin in the Place of Fullness.
> This spirit, the *pneuma*, was the true person (p. 109).

The issue of all Gnosis (and of every Gnosticism) is indeed
"the true person." We have an addiction, in the United States,
that involves the quest of an authentic self, in oneself and in the
other person. Our obsessive hunger for "information" is the
shadow side of this quest. The reductionist's question "What is
he or she really like?" now drives our journalism. Hunting for
true selfhood can be fool's gold; reality recedes as rapidly as we

grasp after it. Searching for the historical origins of Gnosticism is rather like that; the closer the scholar approaches, the more elusive the phenomenon seems to become. "Gnosticism" as a term did not exist before the seventeenth century, but we are unable to avoid using it when we ponder this original tendency, or religion, or heresy, or whatever we choose to call it. Despite its rebellion against normative Judaism, or paradoxically because of it, Gnosticism was probably Jewish in origin. With great respect for the late Hans Jonas, whose writings on Gnosticism have influenced me deeply, I go against him on this question. Gnostic Christianity, I suspect, began with Jesus himself, and with the Jewish Christians led by his brother James, after the death of Jesus. If Jesus essentially was a Gnostic, how did he come by this stance? What is it that makes the Gnostic Jesus of *The Gospel of Thomas* so persuasive?

Before the Ebionites, or Jewish Christians, existed, there were Jewish traditions that exalted Adam as a being higher than the angels, and so as the True Prophet or *Christos,* the Angel Christ. This exaltation seems to me part of the foundation of all Gnosis, including manifestations lost in the abyss of time, in the pre-Yahwist, archaic Jewish religion, of which we necessarily know virtually nothing. Alexandria, by the second century of our era, was the cauldron where Christian Gnosticism was mixed into its varied shapes, as had been the secular Gnosticism of Hermetism, and a still much-disputed Jewish Gnosticism. But the origins of Jewish Gnosticism were not in Alexandria; the rational assumption is that they existed in Palestine. The Christian heresiologists, doubtless for their own polemical purposes, gave what they considered the dubious honor of being the first Gnostic to the Samaritan, Simon Magus, a figure who is no longer easily detached from his extraordinary legend, the story of Faust. As a contemporary of John the Baptist and Jesus, Simon of Samaria shares something of their magical aura. A magus was a magician or miracle worker, and there have been surmises that Simon the magician was, like Jesus, initially a disciple of John the Baptist, perhaps even an overt rival of Jesus the magician.

By the first century before the Common Era, the Jews of Palestine were considerably Hellenized, though not to the extent of the Alexandrian Jews, who spoke Greek and read their Torah in Greek. Perhaps we need a dark formula for explaining Palestinian Jewish Gnosticism, the *minim,* or Gnostic heretics, as the rabbis called them. It is a commonplace to say that, for Palestinian Jewish Gnosticism, failed prophecy was transmuted into apocalyptic expectation: hence the Book of Daniel and the Books of Enoch. What happened to failed Jewish apocalyptics? Evidently, they became Gnostics; thus Gnosticism would have begun as a Jewish heresy, rather than a Christian one. Moshe Idel has surmised that the later Jewish Gnosticism of the medieval Kabbalah was essentially a renewal of ancient Jewish theosophies, particularly of an "ancient Jewish theurgy" for calling down or even strengthening God. In Idel's view, which persuades me, Gnosticism itself, even in its first-century manifestations, was also a return to archaic theosophies. Skeptics who argue against Idel's position like to point out that there are only a handful or so of mysterious references to *minim* by the great rabbis, such as Tarphon and Ishmael, as opposed to the copious invectoriums of early Church fathers devoted to the

Christian Gnostics. This seems to me a tribute to the immense shrewdness of the rabbis, who refused even to mention the heretics, thus hoping to bury them forever. Rabbinical silence, more even than patristic denunciation, was immensely successful in its project to suppress what Idel calls "an inner controversy within Jewish thought."

Yet it remains true that almost all the ancient Gnostic writings we now possess, in whole or in part, represent Christian Gnosticism of the second century of the Common Era. One writer and religious thinker of genius stands out amidst all of the plain bad writing and mythic overfantasizing of most Christian Gnostic literature. This extraordinary figure is Valentinus of Alexandria, who lived from about 100 to 175 C.E. We do not know precisely how Valentinus came to his Gnosticism, or even if he was born a Christian. Bentley Layton, whose *Gnostic Scriptures* (1987) is the best translation of the ancient texts, emphasizes that Valentinus was more of a Gnostic Christian (like Origen, at a later time) than a Christian Gnostic. In Layton's view, Valentinus essentially was a Christian reformer of earlier Gnostic theology. Doubtless, Layton is historically accurate, but the experience of reading Valentinus is distinctly unlike that of reading the Church Fathers, just as the experience of reading the technically non-Gnostic *Gospel of Thomas* is wholly other than that of reading the four Gospels that are canonical. The Jesus of Valentinus is not at all the Christ of Saint Augustine, and the technical monism of Valentinus hardly differs in spirit from Gnostic dualism. From the perspective of a modern common reader, Valentinus is beautifully strange in comparison to New Testament Christianity in its dogmatic or Church development.

Since here I am concerned only with Valentinus's sense of the Resurrection, I will have to neglect many other aspects of the Valentinian Speculation, as Hans Jonas taught us to call it. Very broadly speaking, Christian Gnosticism can be said to have had two phases: so-called Sethian Gnosticism, in which Adam's son Seth becomes the Christ-figure, and the school of Valentinus. Sethian Gnosticism, almost certainly pre-Christian, probably began as a Jewish heresy and then may have merged into Jewish Christianity. Valentinus himself seems to have been acquainted both with Alexandrian Hermetism and with Philo of Alexandria's mystical version of Hellenistic Judaism, so that his Christianity was influenced by many Gnostic or quasi-Gnostic currents.

Resurrection can be judged as one of the sharpest Valentinian differences from dogmatic Christianity, a difference that reappears in Sufism and other esoteric traditions, and in many varieties of what I have called the American Religion, the denominations and sects indigenous to the United States. As in earlier Gnostic religion, resurrection for Valentinus is distinctly *not* something that takes place after death. Henry Corbin, in support of his Sufi Gnostics, quotes from Balzac's novella *Louis Lambert,* itself a Hermetic tale:

> Resurrection is accomplished by the wind of heaven that sweeps the worlds. The Angel carried by the wind does not say: Arise ye dead! He says: Let the living arise!

That is the kernel of the Valentinian resurrection: to *know* releases the spark, and one rises up from the body of this death. Ignorance falls away, one ceases to forget, one is again part of the Fullness. The Valentinian *Gospel According to Philip,* a sort of anthology, has nine crucial passages on resurrection, of which the bluntest insists, "Those who say that the lord first died and then arose are mistaken, for he first arose and then died." Another adds, "While we exist in this world we must acquire resurrection." Baptism, for the Valentinians as for many Americans, itself was the resurrection, again according to *The Gospel of Philip:*

> People who say they will first die and then arise are mistaken. If they do not first receive resurrection while they are alive, once they have died they will receive nothing. Just so it is said of baptism: "Great is baptism!" For if one receives it, one will live.

Only the spark is resurrected, through the liberation of Valentinus's version of baptism. Because his followers, for the five centuries or so that they lasted, were such individual speculators, we have a plethora of Valentinians, but only a few remnants of the master. One of these is a magnificent sermon, *The Gospel of Truth;* the rest are fragments, compressed and enigmatic. One of them seems to come from a sermon preached at Alexandria:

> From the beginning you [of the congregation] have been immortal, and you are children of eternal life. And you wanted death to be allocated to yourselves so that you might spend it and use it up, and that death might die in you and through you. For when you nullify the world and are not

yourselves annihilated, you are lord over creation and all
corruption.

> —translated, like the passages
> following, by Bentley Layton

I wish here to emphasize only the rhetorical authority of
Valentinus. Though a considerable poet, by reputation, his poetry survives only in a single fragment, "Summer Harvest":

> I see in spirit that all are hung
> I know in spirit that all are borne
> Flesh hanging from soul
>
> Soul clinging to air
> Air hanging from upper atmosphere
>
> Crops rushing forth from the deep
> A babe rushing forth from the womb.

"Spirit" means the seer's own spirit, by which he sees and
knows the contingent situation all of us suffer, "hung" from a
soul not our own, but that of the Demiurge, or false god of this
world, who carried us down from our proper place in the divine
Fullness to our confined position in the world of the Creation-
Fall. Yet the Demiurge's soul itself is contingent, pathetically
clinging to the air of the original Fullness, generally named as
the Pleroma. The air itself is fixed in space, hanging from the
upper atmosphere or innermost Pleroma, now closed to us. Yet
the ultimate source of crops, of all fecundity, remains the deep

or parental abyss, at once foremother and forefather, from which the babe rushes forth into our emptiness. Layton calls this "a cosmological poem" suitable for Advent, but not in the eyes of the ancient Catholic Church, whose Saint Hippolytus of Rome quoted the little poem or fragment as a heretical and blasphemous misreading of Advent. So it seems to me, and though Valentinus frequently is termed a Platonist, "Summer Harvest" implies a subversion both of Plato and of the Bible. The crucial text for understanding Valentinus is the subtlest and fullest we have by him, the beautiful sermon named *The Gospel of Truth,* and I turn to it now seeking what is most central to Valentinus's sense of resurrection.

Layton shrewdly remarks upon the "Gnostic rhetoric" of *The Gospel of Truth,* and notes its spiritual similarity, in atmosphere and in the concept of salvation-resurrection to the proto-Gnostic *Gospel of Thomas,* which I suspect deeply influenced Valentinus. Both works, the sermon and the collection of Jesus' "hidden" sayings, are allied by a wonderful freedom from dogma and from myth, both Christian and Gnostic. In each, there is a directness and a passion that breaks down the barriers of reservations put up by historicizing scholars. We are addressed directly, whether by Valentinus or Jesus, and challenged to see what it is that is all around us, what it is that we already know, even if we do not know that we know.

I quote from Layton's translation of *The Gospel of Truth,* as from his versions of previous Valentinian works or fragments, except that I substitute for Layton's "acquaintance" the word "knowing" for the Gnosis:

It was quite amazing that they were in the father without knowing him and that they alone were able to emanate, inasmuch as they were not able to perceive and recognize the one in whom they were.

"They" are the Gnostic elect, the ironically named "perfect," who were parts of the stranger, or alien God, without knowing him. Their process of salvation begins with their emanation, or outward flight, from the father. Paradoxically, they are sent out precisely in order to realize the misery of their ignorance. In Valentinus's parable of the jars, remarkably akin to Isaac Luria's Kabbalistic vision of the breaking of the vessels fourteen hundred years later, the exiled sparks experience their varied fates in the Creation-Fall:

A great disturbance has come to pass among the jars; for some have leaked dry, some are half full, some are well filled, some have been spilled, some have been washed, and still others broken.

Out of this homely parable there comes forth the terrible vision of our nightmare, to be cured only by our waking up. That awakening *is* resurrection, accomplished in *The Gospel of Truth* with a marvelous quietness, through a rhetoric of a widening circle of awareness, a renewal of knowing the estranged father. The father's intervention, through the angelic figure of Jesus, emanates outward again in waves of knowing, until the conclusion of Valentinus's own knowing of "repose," or resurrection, the reentry into the place of Fullness, the original Pleroma:

> This is the place of the blessed. This is their place. As for the others, then, let them know in their own places that it is not right for me to say more, for I have been in the place of repose.

This majestic certitude of having experienced resurrection receives its exegesis in the surviving writings of Valentinus's disciples, particularly in the epistle known as the *Treatise on Resurrection*, which may date from about two centuries after the death of Valentinus. Here the subtle poem of "repose" that was Valentinus's vision of the resurrection becomes somewhat literalized, but the loss is compensated by our realization of how the Valentinians understood their founder's Christian revision of Gnosticism, a revision that by the seventh century was obliterated by the persecuting church. The *Treatise on Resurrection* attempts to explain, rather reductively, Valentinus's threefold sense of resurrection. Our bodies go back to dust; our souls will survive, and will preserve our individualities; our inner selves, or sparks, will return to the Pleroma of the foremother/forefather. The middle term in Valentinian Gnosticism is the most difficult: our souls, made by the Demiurge, are far inferior to our selves, which are as old as God and so not created by him. What is the difference between the fate of the soul, which will not perish, and yet also will not go home to the Pleroma of the uncreated? The soul does not accompany the self to the place of repose, but remains in "the places that are in the middle," the worlds of the *psyche*. Though the *psyche* does not die, it is surrounded by death until it receives a new body of "spiritual flesh," with which it can ascend. This "spiritual" Resurrection Body we have encountered before, among the Sufis, who clearly had Valentinian antecedents in the eclectic backgrounds of their esotericisms. The *Treatise on Resurrection* sums this up with a certain impatience, a conviction that the puzzles of soul and of self already have been worked through:

> Therefore do not concentrate on particulars, O Rheginus, nor live according to (the dictates of) this flesh; do not, for the sake of unity. Rather, leave the state of dispersion and bondage, and then you already have resurrection. For if the dying part (flesh) "knows itself," and knows that since it is moribund it is rushing toward this outcome (death) even if it has lived many years in the present life, why do you (the intellect) not examine your own self and see that you have arisen? And you are rushing toward this outcome (that is, separation from the body) since you possess resurrection.

This is a touch helter-skelter, and does not confront directly Valentinus's subtle evasion of these difficulties. The "perfect" self reenters the Pleroma; the imperfect but redeemed soul, being created, cannot go back to the primal Abyss, but its more limited salvation also proceeds by a gain in knowing. Its resurrection cannot be realized in this life, as can the resurrection of the fully knowing self, but it will be transfigured after death, and thus surmount its origins. Valentinus, a great elitist, offered an intellectual salvation and resurrection to intellectuals, and a modified hope to those of lesser gifts. Doubtless, the ultimate defeat of Valentinianism by the Church, a defeat that prevails until this day, owed much to this spiritual elitism, which baffled ordinary Christians who could not believe that they were already resurrected.

SUFISM: ANGEL OF EARTH AND GARMENT OF LIGHT

Sufism, or Islamic mysticism, is a bewildering labyrinth, and yet one of its traditions, Shi'ite Gnosticism, has a particular power of illumination as we approach Millennium. Two of Sufism's greatest scholars, Henry Corbin and Annemarie Schimmel, agree upon the starting point for this esoteric discipline. In Sura 7:171 of the Koran, God—*before* he creates Adam—calls forth from Adam's uncreated loins all of humanity-to-be and demands of them: "Am I not your Lord?" to which all of us reply: "Yes, we bear witness to it!" This is the primordial Covenant between the divine and the human, preceding the covenants of Noah, Abraham, Moses, Jesus, and Muhammad himself, whose prophecy reconfirms this initial exchange. Sufism, Schimmel comments, seeks to return us to the day of the first covenant, when God existed in perfect solitude, except for his book, the Koran, which was also uncreated and so was as eternal as God. Hallaj, a tenth-century Sufi martyr, identified knowledge of the

Koran with the angelic state of resurrection: "Whoever knows the Koran already is the resurrection." "Knows" is the crucial term here, equating Gnosis and resurrection.

Henry Corbin returns frequently in his books to the symbolic figure of Fatima, daughter of the prophet Muhammad and wife of Ali, the martyred first imam of the Shi'ites. Fatima, rather superbly known as "the dazzling," is for the Iranian Sufis the Angel of Earth of the Celestial Earth, and so a transcendent being, part of the heavenly Pleroma (Fullness) as well as a historical person. I have mentioned Hurqalya, the World of the Celestial Earth earlier in this book, but return to it now for a somewhat fuller exposition, since the Gnosis set forth by Corbin depends upon it as a fundamental context or imaginal setting for spiritual vision. Expounding Hurqalya, Corbin can sound rather like a literary critic analyzing a fantasyland in a work of romance or science fiction:

> The spiritual universe of Iran, before and after the advent of Islam, here becomes of the greatest importance. In its recurrent expressions (Zoroastrianism, Manicheism, Hermetism, and Sufism) this Figure [of Hurqalya] points in one direction: to the light of the North as the threshold of the beyond, to the dwellings in the high North which are the inner abodes secreting their own light. The mystic Orient, the Orient-origin, is the *heavenly pole,* the point of orientation of the spiritual ascent acting as a magnet to draw beings established in their eternal haecceity toward the palaces ablaze with immaterial matter. This is a region without any coordinates on our maps: the paradise of Yima, the Earth of Light, *Terra lucida,* the heavenly Earth of *Hurqalya.*

That "North" is not to be found on any map, but is the threshold of the beyond, the imaginal gateway to the divine world. The light arising in that North is the luminous "black light" of a kind of midnight sun. These optics, like the geography, belong to the angelic world, a transmutation of the Platonic Ideas into Iranian mythology, which has an extraordinary continuity between ancient Zoroastrianism and Shi'ite Islam. Fatima, Corbin remarks, is a figure both of initiation and of transcendence, and the journey to the cosmic North is a Gnostic ritual of initiation. Doubtless the Jungians would see this as a psychic reintegration, but I am interested, in this book, in the spiritual superiority of older Gnosis to our debased contemporary modes, whether cultic or popular. Corbin urges us to distinguish Hurqalya as "the place of transfigurations" from those scenes of demonic or twilight fantasy that are the staple of our New Age phantasmagorias. Here is Corbin's translation of the Sufi sage Suhrawardi (martyred in 1191), in his *Book of Oriental Theosophy:*

> The suprasensory realities encountered by the prophets, the Initiates, and others appear to them sometimes in the form of lines of writing, sometimes in the hearing of a voice which may be gentle and sweet and which can also be terrifying. Sometimes they see human forms of extreme beauty who speak to them in most beautiful words and converse with them intimately about the invisible world; at other times these forms appear to them like those delicate figures proceeding from the most refined art of the painters. On occasion they are shown as if in an enclosure; at other times the forms and figures appear suspended. Everything which is

perceived in dream—mountains, oceans, and continents, extraordinary voices, human personages—all these are so many figures and forms which are self-subsistent and need no substratum. The same is true of perfumes, colors, and flavors. How can the brain, or one of its cavities, contain the mountains and oceans seen in a dream, whether the dream be true or false, no matter how one conceives of, or explains, this capacity? Just as the sleeper on awakening from his dreams, or the imaginative man and the contemplative man, between the waking state and sleep, returning from their vision, leave the world of autonomous Images without having to make any movement or without having the feeling of material distance in relation to it, in the same way he who dies to this world meets the vision of the world of Light without having to make any movement because he himself is in the world of Light. . . .

I cannot say that this powerful passage is simple, but I find it astonishingly lucid, and it has the authority of its spiritual distinction to carry the reader past at least some of its subtle difficulties. The two crucial phrases are "the world of autonomous Images" and "the world of Light," the first world being Hurqalya and the second the cosmic North. What is astonishingly beautiful is the parallel that Suhrawardi sketches, between the exemplary Images and the divine Light, *not in regard to one another* but in the ease, the lack of movement, that constitutes transmutation or transfiguration, as the sleeper wakes up from his dream, the imaginative man returns from his vision, and the Gnostic, dying to this world, finds he is already in the world of Light. No movement need be made, whether by the sleeper waking up, the sage withdrawing from Hurqalya, or the fully initiated mystic perceiving a Light in which he himself already dwells. If you look back at Suhrawardi's "suprasensory realities," you come to see how diverse they are, in kind and in degree. These "autonomous Images" are party aesthetic, partly visionary, because Hurqalya participates in both modes of apprehension. It is, as Corbin says, an *interworld,* located both at the "high point of Time" and at the lowest degree of Eternity. Like the realms represented in painting and in poetry, Hurqalya thrives on its contradictions, because like them it is a world of Images. Hurqalya's Images, however, according to Corbin's sages, are *prior* to the creations of painters and poets. They go back to Ibn 'Arabi's wonderful recital that gave us an "Earth of True Reality," whose emblem is the palm tree, "Adam's sister." From the clay left over from the creation of Adam, there was fashioned both the palm tree and the Earth of Truth, the Earth of Hurqalya, of which Fatima is the presiding archangel, equivalent to the Sophia of the early Gnostics. Concerning this Earth of Truth, Ibn 'Arabi says it is not the place where the soul merges itself with God, but rather where the soul sees itself as an angel might see it, alone in itself and with itself, wholly at peace. Hurqalya, intermediate world as it is, is a place of passage, whether for visionaries ascending from below or angels descending from above. What takes place in Hurqalya goes beyond common empirical perception and yet is still individualized as purely personal vision, unlike the angelic world. Corbin sums it up in a lucid formula: *Hurqalya is the Earth of the soul, because it is the soul's vision.*

That means we gain entry to Hurqalya only by opening our

souls to vision, here on our common earth. To cite again the Jesus of *The Gospel of Thomas:* "The kingdom is inside you and it is outside you." Nothing need mediate your deepest self or innermost soul; everything is open to you, you need but knock and enter. We do not see the kingdom, called Hurqalya by the Sufi sages, but nevertheless it is spread out upon the earth. When it is perceived, it becomes, for the Gnostic Jesus and the Sufis alike, the "earth of Resurrection," where "the Resurrection Body," as described earlier in this book (see p. 162) thrives. Yet so far I have followed Corbin only in giving an account of Hurqalya as the domain of Fatima, the Angel of Earth. To complete the account, I need to chart the human entrance into the world of Hurqalya's images, an entrance made by the agent Corbin calls both "the Man of Light" and "the Garment of Light." This Man or Garment is simply the seeing soul, not acting as a witness of an event external to itself but as the veritable medium in which the event takes place.

And yet, as all gnostic traditions add, there must also be a guide for the Man of Light, an alter ego or guardian angel, who is distinct from the soul in the intermediate realm, though not wholly distinct in the higher regions. Expounding Suhrawardi's system, Corbin invokes the idea of "Perfect Nature" from the Hermetic Corpus and the Arabic Hermetism that it inspired. As ought to be expected in a tradition as eclectic as Gnosticism, the Hermetic Perfect Nature takes on many guises and manifestations throughout the centuries, including a Neoplatonized Prometheus and the "Man of Light" who speaks through the mouth of Mary Magdalene in the Gnostic *Pistis Sophia* as she takes part in the conversations between the resurrected Jesus and his disciples. In all these occurrences, a four-termed analogical structure needs to be noted, as it is here by Corbin:

> "The power which is in thee," in *each one* of you, cannot refer to a collective guide, to a manifestation and a relationship collectively identical for *each one* of the souls of Light. . . . The infinite price attached to spiritual individuality makes it inconceivable that salvation could consist in its absorption into a totality, even a mystical one. What is important is to see that it refers to an analogical relationship presupposing *four* terms, and this essentially is just what is so admirably expressed in the angelology of Valentinian Gnosis: Christ's Angels are Christ himself, because each Angel *is* Christ related to individual existence. What Christ is for the souls of Light as a whole, each Angel is for each soul. Every time one of these conjunctions of soul and Angel takes place, the relationship which constitutes the pleroma of Light is reproduced.
>
> —*The Man of Light in Iranian Sufism*
> (translated by Nancy Pearson, 1978), p. 16

"What Christ is for the souls of Light as a whole, each Angel is for each soul": by this Corbin means not the Christ of the Incarnation, as in Pauline doctrine, but the Angel Christ of the Gnostics, who was not crucified and who was resurrected from the Baptism onwards. The Angel Christ stands to all Light-seeking souls precisely as the angel guide is for each Man of Light. Each soul is a Hermes, each guide his Perfect Nature.

Putting on the Perfect Nature is to be clothed by the angel not *in,* but *as,* a Garment of Light. Stemming as it does from the Manichaean transmutation of Gnosticism, this Sufi vision seems to me much the best corrective we all of us could have to the softness of our current popular, commercialized angelology. The image of the angel can be of use to us only insofar as we are capable of seeking Gnosis, by a hard path of spiritual rebirth. Our popular cult of angels patronizes those formidable beings. Better to remember the tradition that when Muhammad the prophet asked to gaze upon Gabriel, the angel of his revelation, the petition was granted but then caused the prophet to faint away, so shocked was he to see the angel crowding the horizon, and stretching above the prophet's view, so that the giant form filled all space. What we make into an empty image could still retain its enormous power, but only if approached again with all the powers of the mind and spirit.

THE KABBALAH: METATRON, THE LESSER YAHWEH

Several times earlier in this book, I have discussed Metatron, the Kabbalistic Angel of the Divine Presence, who is the transmogrified patriarch Enoch. Since "God took him" without his dying, Enoch-Metatron presumably occupied the imagination of the rabbinical sages long before the formal origins of the Kabbalah, before even the Maccabean era, in which the Books of Enoch were composed. Yet the Babylonian Talmud, which introduced most of the Jewish names for the angels, is anxiously sparse in its references to Metatron, while making clear that his functions include "heavenly scribe" and "guide," attributes of the Greek Hermes and the Egyptian Thoth, brought together later in Alexandria in the Hermetic Corpus as the fused figure of a Gnostic Hermes. Scholem emphasizes that the Talmudic Metatron tends to be mentioned in contexts where the sages are denouncing heretics, the *minim* who may have been the first Jewish dualists, or Gnostics. Elisha ben Abuyah, invariably attacked by the normative rabbis as the very archetype of heresy, was known by them under the nickname of Acher, the "other," or "stranger," perhaps because he worshipped the "stranger God" of Gnosticism. Elisha saw Metatron seated on a throne, in a vision of Heaven, and thus was moved to the observation: "Perhaps there are two Gods in Heaven." The Talmud held that Metatron subsequently was punished by sixty strokes of a flaming rod, so as to remind him that he was only an angel, and presumably also to encourage the others—an instructive vision of the heavenly court as a kind of immortal Singapore which clearly manifests a rabbinic anxiety.

Another Talmudic passage identifies Metatron with the angel of Exodus 23:21, who teaches Moses to ascend to God, and who shares in the name of Yahweh. Metatron, here as elsewhere, rather dangerously takes on some of the creative attributes of God, and is a primordial or originary being, existing before the creation of the world. It is all too easy to assimilate this aspect of Metatron to the Anthropos or primordial Adam, who became the Adam Kadmon, or Divine Man, of the Kabbalists. A fascinating complexity came into play when this Metatron as "lesser Yahweh," or Anthropos, became attached to the undying Enoch of the apocalyptic literature, an assimilation however totally ignored in the Talmud and in other rabbinical writings. This translation of Enoch into Metatron is after all most mysterious: how could Metatron have existed before the foundation of the world and also be the consequence of the apotheosis of a patriarch in Genesis?

What clearly is the answer suggests how much normative censorship was at work both in the Bible and in the Talmud. The J Writer, or Yahwist, a great imaginer and an ironist, is not likely to have confined an account of Enoch to the highly elliptical: "And Enoch walked with Yahweh and Yahweh took him, for he was not." Something crucial is missing there; what did it mean to walk with Yahweh, so long before Abram (Abraham) walked with him? I think that this was the J Writer's metaphor for being as early or as old as Yahweh, as originary as Yahweh. Enoch was Divine Man, or Adam-as-God, and he did not *become* Metatron; the Kabbalistic formula states: "Enoch *is* Metatron." We still do not know what the name Metatron meant; we do not even know its etymology. The Books of Enoch speak of the angels as the Watchers, and there could be a link between *nator*, "watch over," and Metatron. Rather more likely, the name could be Greek, derived from *meta thronon*, or "beyond the throne." Kabbalistically, the name sometimes is ascribed to its numerical value, equal to *Shaddai*, the name of God considered as beyond measure in power. Whatever the origin of his name, Metatron is the central angel of Western tradition, both heterodox and orthodox, though he goes under an extraordinary variety of names, depending upon which tradition is involved. In an earlier version, he sometimes was called Jahoel, the name under which he appears in some Gnostic texts. Early heterodox Jewish works tend to substitute Metatron for the archangel Michael. Later Kabbalah returned to anthropomorphic speculations in order to posit two Metatrons, one spelled with six, the other with seven letters: the six-lettered Metatron is Enoch, the seven is the lesser Yahweh. This equivocation was another quasi-normative evasion, since the ascent of Enoch indeed is the restoration of the Anthropos, or Adam Kadmon, an identification central to Kabbalah.

Gershom Scholem's great revisionist successor, Moshe Idel, pioneered a speculation central to the argument of this book, which is that Jewish Gnosticism *may* be older than "normative" (that is, Platonized) Judaism. If Jewish Gnosticism *was* pre-Hellenistic, then it *may* go back to an archaic Jewish speculation that was Hermetic before Alexandrian Hermetism, back to an Adam-as-God vision of a primal Anthropos who terrified the angels. The acute scholar of Valentinian Gnosticism, Bentley Layton, thinks that Valentinus "reformed" an earlier Gnosticism into Christian Gnosticism, making its harsh dualism into a quasi-monism. But Valentinus may have come out of Jewish Alexandria, and thus could be recalling a Gnosticism *before* Gnosticism, a Jewish Hermetism half a millennium older than pagan Hermetism. I myself, in my *Book of J,* emphasized that the Yahwist is neither "normative" nor "Gnostic," possibly because the elite under Solomon had become skeptical, ironical urbanites. It comes down to the central argument of this book: Was God originally anything more than the Adam Kadmon? Is not the J Writer's Yahweh more a man than an angel, even as he also is more an angel than God? The Gnostic myth of the Anthropos evidently was part of an archaic Jewish religion, censored out of existence in the redacted Hebrew Bible, but surviving in the figure variously called Enoch, Metatron, Hermes, Idris, or what you will.

Elliot R. Wolfson, in a recent study, *Through a Speculum That Shines* (1994), expounds Metatron as he figures in the extraordinary vision of Eleazar of Worms (1165–1230), a leading mystic of the Jewish Pietists of the Rhineland. For these Pietists, Metatron was at once the *Shekhinah* (the feminine indwelling presence of God in the world) and also the outgoing presence of God *in the form of a man*, the angel as a giant human body. Indeed, the guises of Metatron throughout Jewish tradition are extraordinarily varied: sometimes he is identified as the rainbow that concludes Noah's flood, or as the back of God mentioned in Exodus 33:20, or as Ezekiel's chariot, or as the cherub who sits on God's throne, or even as the phallus of God. One can venture that Metatron gathers up all those images of God that normative Judaism tended to reject but that nevertheless could not be excluded from Jewish traditions. Earlier in this book, introducing Metatron, I cited Moshe Idel's suggestion that Metatron, as the apotheosis of Enoch, represented the restoration of the Anthropos, or Primordial Adam, who had come apart in the Creation-Fall. Hidden in the figure of Metatron is the Anthropos, a lost element in archaic Jewish religion, in whatever it was that preceded the earliest layers of what was to become Scripture. The most frequent title of Metatron, "Prince of the Countenance," is itself ambiguous. In the Ethiopic Book of Enoch, Metatron is one of the angels allowed to behold the face of God, but later, as "Prince of the Countenance," he seems to share in what he beholds. This ambiguity preludes other contradictory aspects of this greatest of the Judaic angels. Sometimes Metatron is called the heavenly scribe, recording our deeds; yet his role varies. He can be our defense attorney in the heavenly court, or a minister of the throne. None of these functions sorts easily with his appearance as the *na'ar*, a "youth" or servant with a celestial tabernacle all his own. When later he takes the place of Michael as the prime archangel, that adds yet another confusion to his mingled identities. But there is much more: Metatron became the crucial angel of Kabbalah, because he alone was believed to know all the secrets of the *Merkabah*, the Divine Chariot described by Ezekiel, and by a long tradition of ecstatic visionaries after him. As the master of all the hidden mysteries of Torah, Metatron became the patron of the *Zohar*, the central book of books of classical Kabbalah.

The Kabbalah: Luria's Transmigration of Souls

The great normative rabbis, the Sages of the Oral Law, as Ephraim E. Urbach calls them in his massive *The Sages: Their Concepts and Beliefs* (translated into English, 1975), were far more interested in redemption than in resurrection, though they held to a belief in the resurrection of the body. They were not however much exercised about that belief, except when it was either denied by Jews they termed "Epicureans" or by Jewish Gnostics who had contempt for the normative view that the body and soul originally were unified. On the question of the Messiah (or Messiahs) the Sages differed widely. My own favorite among their stances is Rabba's outcry: "Let him come, but may I not see him!" Esoteric versions of resurrection, including Platonic transmigration of souls, were definitely excluded by the canny Sages. They greatly preferred to think about the redemption of Israel, a communal aspiration, and one they sensibly regarded as a very gradual process.

I am divided, always, between a normative remnant within myself and a personal passion for Gnosis, so I abandon the Sages for the Kabbalists with certain nostalgic regrets. But this is a book about Gnosis in the shadow of Millennium, and the Sages are antithetical to my subject. For the Kabbalists, the question of resurrection was answered by the doctrine of the transmigration of souls, which in turn depended upon the Kabbalah's vision of the soul itself. That vision, except for some of its refinements, was not Judaic but rather Platonist, which is true also of the Sufi account of the soul. The Hebrew Bible has no separate sense of the soul as apart from the body. In the Yahwistic account of the Creation (Genesis 2:7) we are told that "man became a living soul [*nephesh*]," where *nephesh* is not the *psyche* but the whole man. When the Book of Job (12:10) says, "In whose hand is the soul [*nephesh*] of every living thing, and the breath [*ru'ah*] of all mankind," the *ru'ah* is not separate from the soul but is a power energizing it. Yet even the Sages become Platonized enough to separate the soul from the body, and to see them as now antithetical to one another. Nearly a thousand years later, living in a Muslim world order, the rabbis accepted an Arabic, Neoplatonized version of Aristotle, and so adopted the doctrine of a tripartite soul: *nephesh, ru'ah,* and *neshamah,* respectively the natural soul, the transcendent faculty, and the spirit proper, which is attained through Torah study and can become an intuitive link to God. The Neoplatonist Abraham Ibn Ezra, who helped formulate this Hebrew version of a tripartite soul, might have been astonished to see what the Kabbalists made of it, a fantasy of cosmological scope that culminated in the Lurianic doctrine of metempsychosis, *gilgul,* or the transmigration of souls.

The Kabbalistic *neshamah* is very close to, almost identical with, the Gnostic spark, or *pneuma,* which is no part of the created world, but is as old as God, indeed is part or particle of God. The image of the spark is precisely the same for the Gnostics and the Kabbalists. Whether the two esotericisms go back to common, archaic Jewish sources, as Moshe Idel thinks, or whether the Kabbalah owed much to Islamic Sufism, is still fundamentally undetermined. The earliest extant Kabbalistic work, the book *Bahir* (about 1175–80, from Provence, though perhaps of much earlier origin in some portions), teaches the transmigration of souls in a manner more consonant with Arabic than with Judaic tradition. Gershom Scholem points out that Sunni, or normative Islam, the Catholic Church, and the rabbis and Jewish philosophers all had rejected transmigration, but it had survived among Christian Gnostics, Shi'ite Islam, and at last in the Kabbalah, and in their Provençal contemporaries, the

Cathars or Manichaeans, against whom the French king and Church sent a crusade of extermination.

Gilgul, in its very sound, expresses its original meaning, a "rolling over" of souls according to the Kabbalah. The earliest Kabbalists were fairly explicit in distinguishing rolled-over, or "old," souls from new ones, but Scholem notes a deliberate toning-down of *gilgul* in the classical or Spanish Kabbalists of the thirteenth century. Evidently, in the days of the sage Nachmanides the doctrine went underground, and became a secret knowledge or Gnosis proper. It also became a punishment, not applicable to the righteous, who did not need to experience reincarnation. Still, this was a dialectical punishment, since it could involve Abel's rebirth as Moses, and Cain's reincarnation as Jethro, father-in-law to Moses. This notion of prophetic chains or cycles of transmigration, whether in the Kabbalah or in Shi'ite Sufism, seems to go back to the Jewish Christians or Ebionites, who were an undoubted influence upon the prophet Muhammad. For the Ebionites, the first true prophet was Adam, the final one Jesus, whose legatee was his brother James the Just. Muhammad, in this tradition of prophetic reincarnation, had it revealed to him that *he* was the seal of the prophets, making Jesus only another forerunner, like Adam or like Moses. The Kabbalists, who never ceased to expect a Messiah (like their Hasidic heirs), saw instead a sequence of Adam, King David, and the Messiah, three incarnations of the same soul. But does that imply that only the final incarnation is fully redeemed? Scholem, in his *On the Mystical Shape of the Godhead* (English translation, 1991), asks the question with considerable pungency:

. . . what will become of the various bodies through which a soul has passed when the dead are resurrected? Can one assume, as several Kabbalists did, that only the last body, in which the soul finally proved itself worthy and righteous, will be physically resurrected?

This palpable difficulty, Scholem thinks, was met by the idea called "soul sparks," which held that the soul, in migrating, does not leave its earlier body, but acts like a candle lighting other candles. Soul sparks, once envisioned, led on to the more imaginative notion that any one of us could be the recipient of sparks from more than one other soul. Indeed, each of us could become a veritable anthology of soul sparks, themselves of three kinds: *nephesh, ru'ah, neshamah.* Since we have all fallen away from Adam Kadmon, the primal man-god, the function of transmigration is to mend us, and so mend the original Adam. Of this mending, Isaac Luria (1534–1572) of Safed in Upper Galilee was the essential theoretician. Luria was not a writer, but a messianic figure, whose teachings were almost entirely conversations with his disciples. His mind was the most original in the history of the Kabbalah, and his doctrines, as set forth in the writings of his followers, have deeply influenced Judaism to this day, particularly Hasidism. Everything in Luria's thought moves in a great triple rhythm. God contracts or withdraws himself; this absence brings about the cosmological catastrophe that Luria called the "breaking of the vessels"; human prayer, study, and ecstatic contemplation bring about a mending that yet may restore a shattered world. Luria's greatest originality may have been his accommodation of this sequence to his vision of the transmigration of souls. "Vision" is precise, as applied to Luria; he was famous for his ability to look into the face of a stranger, and to see there all the soul sparks dwelling in that countenance. As much as with the Ba'al Shem Tov, we confront in Luria someone more than a sage or even a religious genius or prophet.

Gershom Scholem believed that the Lurianic reinterpretation of Judaism was a myth of exile, a reaction to the expulsion of the Jews from Spain, just a generation before Luria. And yet Luria was of German Jewish ancestry, and very little concerned with contemporary history. Moshe Idel, disputing Scholem, has urged us to a more pragmatic study of Lurianic Kabbalah, which is simply beyond my learning or my powers. But there is certainly a disproportion between Luria's vast formulations and the hard specificity of the Spanish expulsion, enormous and dreadful catastrophe as that indubitably was (grimly enough, as half a millennium has shown, catastrophic for Spain as well). Luria's concerns are as exalted and supernal as any in spiritual history; like those of Valentinus and the Sufi masters, they deal with the inner life of God, as well as with the redemption of the soul. Since all our souls, according to Luria, were once components of Adam's soul, for Luria our authentic catastrophe is Adam's fall, hardly a surprising notion in Augustinian Christianity, but peculiar in a Judaic context. Adam was intended by God to be a mending agent, restoring the broken vessels of the Creation, and Adam's failure therefore showered soul sparks in all directions: some back to the higher realms, some deeper within Adam himself, and most into the world of the broken vessels, the sensible emptiness of our lives. Luria names these the "great souls," each of which can contain as many as a thousand individual sparks or souls. Great souls can be redeemed, and sometimes are redeemed, but only by the holy efforts of their individual components. Yet you can raise only a spark to which you are innately allied, which certainly does not mean by a familial bond. Luria fascinatingly taught that parents and children almost never have an affinity of sparks, almost never share the same root. So much for Freudian psychology! Luria makes however a shocking exception: the souls of Adam that survived within him were passed down both to Cain and Abel. Cain, a hero to at least some early Gnostics, is again exalted by Lurianic Kabbalah, and receives prophetic status, an eminence that Lord Byron, author of *Cain: A Mystery,* would have appreciated, but hardly what we would expect from normative Judaism.

This might suggest that the transmigration of souls, for Luria, was a process that took one beyond good and evil. "Raising the sparks" seems to have been an esoteric quest, rather than a conventionally moral one. It is difficult for me anyway to see how ordinary ideas of virtue could aid much in redeeming the sparks, since each of us is complexly involved with souls that we might find highly uncongenial were we to encounter them in daily life. There is a superb anarchy in Luria's intimation that many surprises await us in our efforts to lift up the other sparks that stem from our own root. Clearly, we have very little insight into either others or ourselves, unless we are inspired figures like Luria, or like the Ba'al Shem Tov, who insisted that God sees to it that we *will* encounter all the sparks of our own soul, perhaps whether we wish this or not. Yet the antinomian possibilities of the Lurianic idea, which were alien to Hasidism, had burgeoned forth a century after Luria's death in the catastrophic movement of the false Messiah Shabbatai Zevi, who converted to Islam to save his life. Shabbatai's "prophet," Nathan of Gaza, brilliantly reversed Luria by insisting that God's own nihilizing or unforming light had created the monster (*golem*) of the abyss. There, in the depths of the broken vessels, dragons appear, and there the soul of Shabbatai is also manifested. Nathan fiercely proclaims what Luria would have considered blasphemy:

> Know that the soul of the messianic king exists in the lower *golem*. For just as the primal dragon emerged in the vacant space, even so the soul of the messiah was created by the will of God. This soul existed before the creation of the world, and it remains in the great abyss.

The (false) Messiah's apostasy to Islam is the ultimate attempt to raise the sparks of one's own root, presumably by causing the dragons to ascend. Redemption through abasement could not go farther. Doubtless, Nathan of Gaza has to be considered a parody of Lurianic Kabbalah, but he radiates his own nihilizing light upon the transmigration of souls as the path of redemption, whether for an individual or for a community. For Nathan of Gaza, as for Luria, if the sparks are everywhere (in Hasidism, they can be found in your frying pan), then there is no clear object for our more transcendental desires. Nor are our individualities at all clearly defined. Each of us may possess several souls (*neshamah*) of the same root, and no single one necessarily is the most authentic. Since, according to Lurianic Kabbalah, the *nephesh* suffers the punishment of the grave, and always abides there, resurrection depends upon the other aspects of the soul. The *ru'ah* also sustains judgment, and deserved suffering, but only for a year, and then enters the earthly paradise, a restored Garden of Eden. But the *neshamah* ascends to the supernal paradise, because as the true spark it is divine and sinless. Even in the higher paradise, the *neshamah* keeps its identity and does not merge with God. But which *neshamah*, if we have several? The Kabbalah, in almost all of its versions, including the Lurianic, insists that the dead at last will arise, when the time of redemption is accomplished. But the unresolved tension, even potential conflict, between a vision of judgment and the doctrine of transmigration, with its multiple soul sparks, produced enormous contradictions in Lurianic Kabbalah and in its descendants, whether antinomian Shabbateanism or normative Hasidism. Kabbalah, with all its speculative grandeur, nevertheless could not resolve its tangle of curiously mixed sources: ancient Jewish theurgies, Neoplatonism, Gnosticism, Sufism, and perhaps even Christian elements, wholly transformed. There is something irreconcilable in the ideas of transmigration and of Judaic judgment. Shi'ite Sufism, despite its imaginative boldness, nevertheless conveys a more unified image of resurrection than the wilder Kabbalah was able to accomplish.

CHAPTER 5

MILLENNIUM

AMERICAN CENTURIES

One of the many unhappy oddities of the contemporary United States is that so many of us are Bible-obsessed yet have never read the Bible. This has much to do with the phenomenon of Fundamentalism, which insists that the Bible is inerrant, while for the most part declining the difficult labor of reading and interpreting its text. Pollsters estimate that there are about 10 million premillennialists among us, that is, people who expect Jesus to return, in his resurrected body, before he then inaugurates a thousand-year kingdom on earth, over which he will rule. Yet the premillennialists are only a small fraction of believers; rather more than 100 million American adults expect a Second Coming of Jesus, even if they do not necessarily believe that he will found the Kingdom of God in this world. Paul Boyer's *When Time Shall Be No More* (1992) is the most acute study of the prevalence of what he calls "prophecy belief in modern American culture," a mode that compounds itself (as I write) with the future-shock cyberspace apocalypticism of the leader who is taking us into the Age of Gingrich. The alliance between the Christian Coalition of Ralph Reed and Newt, visionary of the New Information, is (alas) soundly based upon their mutual millenarianism. It may be that Gingrich's principal effect upon his prophecy-inspired supporters is that he has reversed their attitude towards computers, since many of them began with the somewhat mad equation that the computer equals Antichrist. Under the sway of the ingenious Speaker, most of them have reversed that early identification, and some now program their prophecies directly upon their laptops.

Jewish apocalyptic writings, though they inaugurated both Christian and Muslim millenarianism, did not invent this visionary mode, and it still retains traces of its Zoroastrian origins, best expounded by Norman Cohn, as I have observed earlier in this study. Cohn shrewdly notes that there are no Jewish denunciations of Persia, whether in biblical or rabbinic texts, whereas Babylon, Greece, and Rome frequently are cursed. Zoroastrians and Jews lived amiably side by side throughout the Hellenistic world, bound together by their mutual grievances against Alexander the Great's successors, including the tyrant Antiochus Epiphanes, against whom the Maccabees rebelled, which was the politico-religious provocation for the earlier Jewish apocalypses, the Book of Daniel and the Books of Enoch. When, in the second century B.C.E., a rejuvenated Iran,

Parthia, momentarily ousted the Romans from Jerusalem, the Zoroastrian-Jewish friendship was intensified. Though the Pharisees, ancestors of what we now regard as normative Judaism, may not have known how influenced they were by Zoroastrianism, nevertheless they imported into their Yahwism crucial elements totally unknown to the Hebrew Bible, yet commonplace in Persia. The bodily resurrection of the dead at a final judgment, after sojourns in Heaven or Hell, was transmitted by the Pharisees to early Christianity, and yet it still seems a foreign concept to many trusting Jews today, though not to most believing Christians and Muslims. Cohn carefully notes that the Pharisees did not absorb the Zoroastrian dualism, with its fierce figure of a power of evil opposed to God. And yet apocalyptic Jews absorbed precisely that, as we can see from Qumran (the Dead Sea Scrolls) or from what may have been Jewish Gnostic groups, and most decisively from the first Christians, who certainly manifested a Zoroastrian dualism.

I think that our contemporary American omens of Millennium reflect the peculiar nature of indigenous American Christianity, which since about 1800 has been rather more Gnostic than orthodox in its temper. As the twenty-first Christian century approaches, our millenarian omens sometimes appear to stage a return to Zoroastrian origins. Herman Melville in *Moby-Dick,* the most apocalyptic of major American novels, astonishingly prophesied just such a return when he portrayed Captain Ahab not as a Quaker Christian (which Ahab must have been in his youth) but as a Zoroastrian fire-worshipper, whose own whaling boat is staffed by Fedallah and other Parsis, still the world's last Zoroastrians. Ahab's great outcry ("I'd strike the sun if it insulted me!) rings on as the ethos of the current United States. Our aggressive millenarianism has very little to do with Christian humility, and can be interpreted as a throwback more to the ancient Iranian sense of being the Chosen People than to the biblical sense of election. It was, after all, Zoroaster, and not the Hebrew prophets, who invented the Western ideas of Hell and of the Devil, and so it is Zoroaster who is the ultimate ancestor of the full range of recent American millenarians, from the now-benign national icon, Billy Graham, all the way to such nativist fascist groups as the Aryan Nation and the Posse Comitatus, unknowing heirs of the ancient Persians.

The healthiest antidote for American millennialism might be a return, by mainline Protestants and Catholics alike, to the theology of Saint Augustine, whose *City of God* (426 C.E.) inspired the rejection of millennialism by the Catholic Church at the Council of Ephesus in 431. For Augustine, the church *was* the Millennium already embodied, the true Kingdom of God already established upon earth. But even an Augustinian revival among traditional Protestants and Roman Catholics would be unlikely to affect the vast majority of American religionists, whose faith is apocalyptic, which at first seems strangely at odds with American middle-class morality. Why should the comfortable and the sanctified anticipate the violent raptures of the promised end? My question is not ironic but expresses my authentic puzzlement. Historically, one expects the dispossessed, the "insulted and injured," the victimized, to embrace the expectations of Millennium. Yet in our contemporary America the only half-fearful longing for an apocalyptic fulfillment pervades far more than the Pentecostals, who frequently are lower class, and reaches out to Mormons, conservative Southern Baptists and other Fundamentalists, and the Adventists, among several other rather prosperous creeds. Why should the owners of America desire a supernatural transformation?

If there is a persuasive answer, it must be found in the nature of American religion, particularly in whatever it is that is uniquely American in the national Gnosis (surely it is, as this book partly exists to show, more a Gnosis than a faith or trust or belief). As I have suggested in an earlier book (*The American Religion,* 1992), I am not inclined to discover the roots of our current millennarianism in seventeenth-century colonial America or eighteenth-century revolutionary America. A radical alteration of American religion commenced with the start of the nineteenth century, in a process studied by such historians as Nathan Hatch and Jon Butler. Enormous frontier revivals surged on into the cities, and premillennialism accompanied the revivals. By the 1830s, the weird Millerite movement was in progress, named for a New York Baptist, William Miller, who proclaimed that the Apocalypse would take place in 1843. Since this did not happen, his more advanced disciples revised his calculations (based upon the Book of Daniel) and named the exact day as October 22, 1844. An extraordinary number of Millerites (counting fellow travelers, they *may* have numbered one hundred thousand) wept bitterly as the dawn came up on October 23. Out of this ruin of expectation, such diverse denominations as the Seventh Day Adventists and the more belated Jehovah's Witnesses eventually came into being. Yet we have at least 10 million premillennialists today, and they are Millerites after the non-event, without knowing it. The year 2000–2001 will not be a comfortable year in the United States of America, not because we will experience either rupture or rapture, but because there are extremist groups among the premillennialists, and *their* disappointment could lead to violence. The Aryan Nation and similar fascist apocalyptics could seek to assuage unfulfilled expectations by terrorism, in a familiar psychological pattern.

They of course are a fringe only; the great mass of American premillennialists will not attach their hopes to the specific years 2000 and 2001. No deep student of Mormonism can fail to be impressed by the formidable pragmatism of the Mormon people. They are an organized (highly organized) American Gnostic church, by no means monotheistic and thus still the heirs of the vision of Joseph Smith, greatest and most authentic of American prophets, seers, and revelators. The prophet Joseph, charismatic and fearless, taught a doctrine both Hermetic and Kabbalistic, perhaps even knowing that these were his affinities. There are a plurality of gods, Joseph declared, and the highest God himself was once the man Adam. And there would be a premillennial Kingdom of God upon the earth, centering in America, and ruled over by a Mormon prophet-king in apostolic succession to Joseph, who was himself one and the same person with Enoch. Whether Joseph knew that he was therefore also the angel Metatron (or Michael) and so the lesser Yahweh, we need not doubt. There are more than 9 million Mormons throughout the world today, while there are more than 900 million Roman Catholics. I myself prophesy that this 1:100 ratio will decrease throughout the twenty-first century, though at what rate who can tell? But there is an urgency, a vitalism in Mormonism, that is astonishing. This most American of religions lives on a threshold between this world and Millennium (an undesignated one) and holds on hard both to this world and the next. Their premillenarianism breaks down the discursive dichotomy between man and God, and so helps inaugurate a new sense, at least in America, of fusion between our cosmos and the world to come. *Their* Zion is famously not "a world elsewhere"; it will be built, someday, near Independence, Missouri, according to a prophecy of Joseph Smith. Oddly, the site of the new "city of Enoch" is not in the hands of the Salt Lake City heresiarchs, but belongs to the Reorganized Mormons, invariably ruled over by the direct descendants of the prophet Joseph. For now, the premillennialist Kingdom of God in America centers itself upon Utah and adjoining states, in a belt that runs through to Orange County, California, birthplace of the Reaganite Revolution and unhappily (and symbolically) bankrupt, even as I write.

GNOSIS OF THE WORLD TO COME

Hebrew prophecy was partly moral admonition, best phrased by William Blake as: "If you go on so, the result is so." Such prophecy says: "Turn now!" Failed prophecy, as I have said, becomes apocalyptic, and failed apocalyptic becomes Gnosticism. Not being a prophet, I have no admonitions to utter, and I expect that all the apocalyptic fears, yearnings, and expectations clustering around Millennium will prove to be false. Can there be a Gnosis of the world to come, here and elsewhere, or does authentic Gnosis confine itself to the timeless knowing of one's own deep self?

Knowing the spark that is the inmost self necessarily involves knowing the self's potential. If we are fragments of what once was a Fullness, the Pleroma as ancient Gnostics called it, then we can know what once we were and what we might yet be again. Freud's attempt at a rational therapy emphasized that the ego, albeit partly unconscious, could be strengthened, and indeed could win a partial freedom from the censoriousness of the superego, that agency above the "I." Freudian therapy scarcely has achieved even that modest aim. This short book, *Omens of Millennium,* has been written in the ancient conviction that "what makes us free is the Gnosis." Spiritual freedom answers an acute yearning at the end of an age, even if one does not believe, as I do not, that particular catastrophes await the nation and the world in the year 2000 or 2001. Our popular obsessions with angels, telepathic and prophetic dreams, alien abductions, and "near-death experiences" all have their commercial and crazed debasements, but more than ever they testify to an expectation of release from the burdens of a society that is weary with its sense of belatedness, or "aftering," a malaise that hints to us that we somehow have arrived after the event. William Blake remarked that everything possible to be believed is an image of truth. It is difficult to sustain that observation at the present time, when we are flooded with bizarre beliefs, in a violent America that already suffers from too many apocalyptic obsessions. As a people crazed with an appetite for information, we are natural Gnostics anyway. The American God and the American Jesus are encountered experientially by

American religionists, so many of whom assert intimate acquaintance with God's or Jesus' love for them.

The most authentic omen of the Millennium could be named as our emergent dream of a guardian angel of personal resurrection, since the three most pervasive of current omens—angels, dreams, not dying—meet in that composite image. We have encountered that image in many guises in this book: Metatron of the Kabbalah; the Answering Angel of Joseph Karo's prophetic dreams; the angel stationed at our end in traditions of resurrection; the Divine Man or Perfect Nature of Hermetic lore; the Angel Christ of Christian Gnosticism; the Garment or Man of Light of the great Iranian Sufis. I have offered these versions of the angel of resurrection not so much as a corrective to our popularized accounts, but as an enhancement. It puzzles me that transcendent intimations, once vouchsafed to spiritual adepts and powerful intellects, now seem available mostly to devotees of dank crankeries. My own conviction is that the dogmatic orthodoxies—normative Judaism, the Roman Catholic Church, mainline Protestantism, Sunni Islam, the current Shi'ite regime in Iran—have suppressed or exiled the imaginative element in Western religion, which is the Gnosis whose prophets include Valentinus, Isaac Luria, and Henry Corbin's Shi'ite sages, among those discussed in this book, and the great "heretics" who are not: Meister Eckhart, Jakob Boehme, Swedenborg, William Law, and a host of others, William Blake not least among them.

There always is a world to come, not a world elsewhere, but one to be known here and now. The most universal prophet of this knowing seems the highly heterodox Jesus of *The Gospel of*

Thomas, who thus instructs his disciples, when they ask who will guide them after he leaves:

> No matter where you are, you are to go to James the Just, for whose sake heaven and earth came into being.

I have referred several times earlier in this book to James, who died in the year 62 of the Common Era, and who headed the Jerusalem congregation of Jesus' own family and followers. There are many claimants to that vanished group and its gnosis, including the Gnostics of the *Secret Book of James,* all of Islam, and many Hermetists and esoteric visionaries throughout the more than nineteen centuries that have gone by since James's death. Some have speculated that the sectaries of the Dead Sea Scrolls were disciples of James the Just. I have remarked more than once in this book that I endorse the surmises of those who have identified the congregation of James the Just with a Jewish Gnosticism that preceded Jesus, and to which Jesus adhered, though scholars as eminent as Hans Jonas have doubted that a Jewish Gnosticism ever existed. Erwin Goodenough, a close reader of Philo of Alexandria, reached opposite conclusions, and spoke of "the mystical doctrine of Hellenistic Jewry," both Alexandrian and Palestinian. The Essenes, who *may* be identical either with the community of James the Just or with the Dead Sea Covenanters, or with both, already represented a form of Gnostic thought, since they held that God was inaccessible to man as such. But their God *knew* men (certain men), and could illuminate them. The Essenes go back to 150 B.C.E., and precede any Jewish Christian Gnosticism that we can recognize. Martin Hengel, in his *Judaism and Hellenism* (translated into English, 1974), speaks of the Essenes as being among the earliest "Jewish magicians," exorcising illnesses by their angelic power, rather in the mode of Jesus. In Hengel's fine summation, the Essenes appear as the likely common ancestor of a Jewish Christian Gnosis, associated with Baptist phenomena:

> In one sense the "Hellenized" interpretations of the Essene order by the various ancient writers were not completely mistaken, for precisely in Essenism, Judaism points beyond the narrow context of Palestine; the retreat into the solitariness of the desert unleashed great religious consequences which had their effects on primitive Christianity, the baptist movements in Transjordania and early gnosticism (p. 247).

Elsewhere, Hengel affirms that "the first beginnings of Jewish Gnosticism probably developed in heterodox Jewish Samaritan groups," presumably like the one led by the notorious Simon Magus, but quite possibly also involving John the Baptist. Our ideas of Gnosticism have been debased by many centuries of normative Jewish silence and dogmatic Christian libel, and even Simon Magus may be a victim of Pauline Christian defamation. The enemies of Gnosis were and are triumphant, but only in the organizational and political sense. Historically they seem to have won, but all victories over the spirit remain forever equivocal, and the spark or deepest self is never quite snuffed out. Authentic spirituality in the United States, for nearly two centuries now, is essentially Gnostic. As I have said (and implied) throughout this book, there are many versions of Gnosticism, including a kind of Christianity, which fundamentally tends to exclude the Pauline and Augustinian elements. The United States hardly requires a Gnostic revival: its perpetual revivals are nothing else, sometimes, alas, not altogether for the better. Much of what now passes for normative Judaism (Hasidism included) essentially is Jewish Gnosticism, and I assume that the Shi'ite Sufis of Iran will survive their oppressive new Doctors of the Law. Before preaching a Gnostic sermon as my coda, I am content to give the last word here to Macedonio Fernandez, the legendary (but quite real) Gnostic mentor of Jorge Luis Borges, most playful of all Gnostics, ever:

> "Everything has already been said, everything has been written, everything has been done"—this is what God heard. And He had not yet created the world, nor did anything exist. "This too I've heard," He replied, from the parted old Nothing. And He began.
>
> A Romanian woman once sang to me a popular melody that afterwards I recognized countless times, in various works from various authors of the last four hundred years. Things do not begin, no one would question that. Or at least they do not begin at the moment they're invented. The world was invented old from the beginning.
>
> —*Museo de la Novela de la Eterna,*
> translated by Arthur Nestrovski

CODA:

OT BY FAITH,

NOR BY THE

ANGELS

A GNOSTIC SERMON

What makes us free is the Gnosis

    of who we were

    of what we have become

    of where we were

    of wherein we have been thrown

    of whereto we are hastening

    of what we are being freed

    of what birth really is

    of what rebirth really is

That is a Gnostic credo from the second century C.E., and I intend to preach a sermon upon it in the pages that follow. The burden of my sermon will be in no way conversionary; rather I will seek to show many who read and thus hear me the paradox that they already are Gnostics, "knowers," without consciously knowing it. There are of course indigenous American denominations that have strong Gnostic traces in them: the Mormons, many Pentecostals, some Adventists, a surprising number of moderate Southern Baptists, and a multitude of African-American religionists, some black Baptists among them. But I have no authority to address any of these, and can-

not direct this sermon to them. I speak instead to the un-
churched, to seekers of many kinds, who are too lucid and
spiritually mature to play with New Age and Woodstock toys,
and yet who know, on many levels, what Emerson meant when
he wrote in his notebook that "It is by yourself without ambas-
sador that God speaks to you," and added the deepest truth of
all Gnosticism:

> Were you ever instructed by a wise and eloquent man? Re-
> member then, were not the words that made your blood run
> to your cheeks, that made you tremble or delighted you,—
> did they not sound to you as old as yourself? Was it not truth
> that you knew before, or do you ever expect to be moved
> from the pulpit or from man by anything but plain truth?
> Never. It is God in you that responds to God without, or af-
> firms his own words trembling on the lips of another.

There is the heart of Gnostic knowing, written in America
in 1831, rather than seventeen hundred years before that in
Hellenistic Alexandria. It is in the conviction that Emerson
was right, and that a great many of us are Gnostics without
knowing what it is that we know, that this sermon expounds
Gnosticism as the spiritual alternative available right now to
Christians, Jews, Muslims, and secular humanists. I therefore
wish to avoid immersion in religious history, scholarship, and
theology, but I need to begin with a very minimal presentation
of background if terms such as "Gnosis," "Gnosticism," and
"the Gnostic religion" are to be understood, and if my sermon
is to have any value. Taking the credo above as my text, I will

allow both background and doctrine to emerge directly from each of the nine lines of the ancient formula.

What makes us free is the Gnosis

What makes us free, according to Christian dogma, is knowing the truth, which is Christ's Incarnation, Crucifixion, and Resurrection, and this truth is to be known by faith, the faith that at a moment, both in and out of time, these events once took place. When however we say that what makes us free is Gnosis, or "knowing," then we are Gnostics, and instead of believing that something was and is so (something that would be still different for Jews, and again for Muslims), we rely upon an inward knowledge rather than upon an outward belief. Gnosis is the opposite of ignorance, and not of disbelief. As an ancient Greek word widely used by Jews and Christians, *Gnosis* did not mean knowing that something was so, but rather just knowing someone or something, including knowing God. "Knowing God" has a special twist that makes it the Gnosis: it is a reciprocal process in which God also knows what is best and oldest in you, a spark in you that always has been God's. This means that knowing God is primarily a process of being reminded of what you already know, which is that God never has been wholly external to you, however alienated or estranged he is from the society or even the cosmos in which you dwell.

How, when, and where did such a Gnosis come about? Normative Judaism, dogmatic Christianity, and orthodox, Sunni Islam all regarded and still regard Gnosis as heresy, as something that blasphemes faith in God and in the revelations of that faith proclaimed through Moses, Jesus, and Muhammad. Scholarly controversy flourishes upon the issue of the origins of "the Gnostic heresy," or "the Gnostic religion," as I prefer to call it, but since I am giving a sermon—a declaration, and not an argument—I will settle the controversy for myself, and for any reader primarily concerned with spiritual search, as I am. Gnosticism first rose among the Hellenistic Jews, both of Alexandrian Egypt and Syria-Palestine, a full century or so before Christ. I do not think that it began as a rebellion against the priestly Creator-God of Genesis 1, though eventually it turned into that, and it continues to regard the false Creation of Genesis 1 as the true Fall of men and of women. Rather, these intertestamental (between Old and New Testaments) Jews were seeking to revive a more archaic Jewish religion that the Temple cult had obscured, a religion in which the demarcation between God and mankind was not a fixed barrier. Ancient Jewish myths and theosophies had long anticipated Gnosticism, and these speculations were revived during the formative first century of Jewish Gnosticism. The most important of them concerned the original or Primordial Adam, the Anthropos, or Man, as Greek-speaking Jews called him, a being at once Adam and God, whose enormous body took up the entire cosmos, but who actually transcended the cosmos. Our world, even before it fell (or shrank into the Creation of Genesis 1), *was contained inside the frame of Adam, Anthropos, Man,* who was indistinguishable from God. Hence the Gnosis, in which a single act of personal knowledge at once comprises man knowing God and God knowing man.

What makes us free is the Gnosis
of who we were

Gnosticism, already existent among pre-Christian Jews, naturally became one of the earliest forms of Christianity, and competed with the burgeoning Church of the first two Christian centuries, after which it was politically defeated and so cast out as heresy. The credo I am preaching upon as my text is a second-century C.E. version of the doctrine of the great Christian Gnostic Valentinus, certainly the most powerful writer among the ancient Gnostics. But now I am going to abandon history, except for occasional moments of clarification, as they become necessary. In the first place, the Gnosis makes us free because it is the knowledge of who we were, before that priestly Creation that was actually our Fall from divinity into division and splintering. Who were we, when we were our original selves? What were our faces, before the world was made? What was our power of being, our condition of consciousness, our relation to life? The Gnosis, for two thousand years now, has been a knowledge pragmatically available only to an elite, to those who are initiated, and who are capable of so large a knowing. But the true knowledge of who we were embraces far more than an elite: it returns us to a universal entity that contained all men and all women. We were, all of us, of a double nature, God and Man, with a reciprocity moving between both aspects. Self-knowledge and knowledge of God were in harmony, and none of this was theoretical, but was experiential. The ancient Hermetic Corpus, writings of pagan Alexandrian Gnostics under some Jewish influence, expressed this wonderful sense of the Gnosis of who we were with great eloquence:

> ... the true Man is above even the gods, or at least fully their equal. After all, none of the celestial gods will leave the heavenly frontiers and descend to earth; yet Man ... establishes himself on high without even leaving the earth, so far does his power extend. We must presume then to say that earthly Man is a mortal god, and that the celestial God is an immortal man.

Yet what can it mean to be "a mortal god"? Since Gnosis is the redemption of the "interior man" or "interior woman," inwardness is the heart or center of the mortal godhead. Gnostic inwardness is not to be confused with Freudian or Jungian excursions into the interior, but depends upon an illumination or a revelation, both from within and from without. The images of awakened inwardness, of who we were, of coming out of an intoxication, always emphasize a meeting between inner and outer realities that seek one another's likeness. Freud hoped to strengthen the ego, and Jung masqueraded as a Gnostic, but the integration that is the Gnosis is quite different from the processes of psychoanalysis or analytical psychology. Part of who we were was God, a personal God but transcending what we have become, as we ourselves once were more than we have become. Pragmatically, the Gnosis is a difference that makes a difference, because the quest is to return to a perfect knowledge, at once experiential and intellectual.

What makes us free is the Gnosis
of what we have become

In all of religious literature, I do not know of a more vivid portrait of spiritual depression than the one that Gnosticism renders of the worst parameters of our earthly existence. Ancient Gnostic writings frequently remind me of the cosmos of Shakespeare's most negatively sublime tragedies, *King Lear* and *Macbeth*, and they remind me also of our terrifying inner cities, and of the eroded desolation of so much American landscape. Our existing world is called the *kenoma*, or cosmological emptiness, by the ancient Gnostics: a world of repetitive time, meaningless reproduction, futurelessness, Generation X: then, now, and forever. What we have become is demon ridden, trapped in a sense of fate ruled by hostile angels called *archons*, the princes of our captivity. Walking around Yale one day, I encountered my friend, the eminent scholar of Gnosticism, Bentley Layton, who inquired as to the pained expression on my face. When I told him truthfully that my feet hurt, he sagely lifted up a finger and remarked: "Ah, that is because of the *archon* of shoes!" In the overdetermined world of what we have become, even Gnostic jokes have their usefulness. There is a contemporary sense of anguish as Millennium approaches, one that has its own distinctive flavor, and it is remarkably akin to the Gnostic anguish of two millennia ago. Our current American obsessions with angels, with parapsychological dreams, with the "near-death experience" and its astral-body manifestations: all of these have clear analogues in the formative period of ancient

Gnosticism. What the Gnosis best teaches us, in this matter, is to end our enthusiasm for angels, who according to Gnosticism are not our guardians but our prison wardens.

> What makes us free is the Gnosis
> of where we were

Gnosticism tells us that before the catastrophe of the Creation-Fall, we were in the place of rest, the "Fullness," or the Pleroma, a paradoxical world of tensely vital peace, and of a calm yet active ecstasy, hardly an easy condition to imagine, at least on a perpetual basis. Yet it seems to me the most humane and interesting account of a Heaven or unfallen condition that I have ever encountered. Monoimos, an early Arab Gnostic influenced by archaic Jewish theosophies, gave a witty insight into the Man of the Pleroma, the Unfallen human of the Fullness:

> Cease to seek after God and creation and things like these and seek after yourself of yourself, and learn who it is who appropriates all things within you without exception and says, "*My* God, *my* mind, *my* thought, *my* soul, *my* body," and learn whence comes grief, and rejoicing and love and hatred, and waking without intention, and sleeping without intention, and anger without intention, and love without intention. And if you carefully consider these things, you will find yourself within yourself, being both one and many like that stroke, and will find the outcome of yourself.

"That stroke" marvelously refers to the single stroke of the Greek letter iota, the I, which being numeral as well as letter, stands for the number ten, the number containing all other numbers. And so Monoimos, whom I would call the first Gnostic wit or humorist, goes on to make "that stroke" also the Gnostic stroke of interpretation, seeing the perfect Man in the harmony of the Pleroma:

> This Man is a single unity, incomposite and indivisible, composite and divisible; wholly friendly, wholly peaceable, wholly hostile, wholly at enmity with itself, dissimilar and similar, like some musical harmony, which contains within itself everything which one might name or leave unnoticed, producing all things, generating all things. . . .

In relation to original Man in the Pleroma, our cosmos is a deformed copy, and so are we. We cannot join opposites, unlike the Androgyne, who is Anthropos, and is at once man and woman, God and human, our forefather and our foremother, the root of the tree of our existence. As many contemporary feminists are well aware, the god of the Gnostics long ago voided the absurdity so difficult to remove from Judaism, Christianity, and Islam: the exclusively male Godhead. And there is sexual life within the Androgyne: how could there not be? The story of that sexual life is most developed in the Jewish Kabbalah, but it is present in the Gnosis from its beginnings.

> What makes us free is the Gnosis
> of wherein we have been thrown

"Thrown" is the most important verb in the Gnostic vocabulary, for it describes, now as well as two thousand years ago, our condition: we *have been thrown* into this world, this emptiness. Cast out, at once from God and from our true selves, or sparks, we live and die our sense of having been thrown, daily. Let us grant that there is an exhilarating dynamism in our condition, but this does not prevail, and it is not the norm of our existence. Trauma is far closer to our days and nights: fears of lovelessness, deprivation, madness, and the anticipation of our deaths. Here is Valentinus upon our present state in his one complete surviving work, the beautiful meditation *The Gospel of Truth:*

> Thus they did not know God, since it was he whom they did not see. Inasmuch as he was the object of fear and disturbance and instability and indecisiveness and division, there was much futility at work among them on his account, and much empty ignorance—as when one falls sound asleep and finds oneself in the midst of nightmares: running toward somewhere—powerless to get away while being pursued—in hand-to-hand combat—being beaten—falling from a height—being blown upward by the air, but without any wings; sometimes, too, it seems that one is being murdered, though nobody is giving chase—or killing one's neighbors, with whose blood one is smeared; until, having gone through all these dreams, one awakens.

This nightmare of death-in-life, composed eighteen centuries ago, needs but little modification. The Gnostic Jesus of *The Gospel of Thomas,* a wayfaring Jesus, closer to Walt Whitman than to the Jesus of the Churches, speaks to us as if each of us is a passerby, and with an ultimate eloquence tells us precisely into what we have been thrown:

> But if you do not know yourselves, then you dwell in poverty, and you are poverty.
>
> Fortunate is one who came into being before coming into being.

"Poverty" here is exactly what Ralph Waldo Emerson, founder of our American Gnosis, named as poverty: imaginative lack or need. We came into being before coming into being; we always already were, and so we were never created, being as old as God himself. And yet we have been thrown into that world, our lives, where Jesus advises us to "be passersby."

What makes us free is the Gnosis
of whereto we are hastening

If we have been thrown, who was the thrower? There is no Odin or Jupiter or Yahweh who by himself has thrown us out of the Pleroma: it can only be by the aid of oneself. Rather, it was and is not the self, spark, or *pneuma* (to use the Gnostic word) but is the *psyche,* or soul, the shallower companion of the deeper self. As we live day to day, we experience, by glimmers, a sense of whereto we are hastening, but it is the retrospective view that hurts us most. At sixty-five, I frequently find myself bewildered by my own question: Where have the years gone? As I write this sermon, I am about to commence teaching my fortieth consecutive year at Yale, and cannot sustain in my consciousness the speed at which forty years departed. Yet my experience is all but universal, among my friends and acquaintances in my own generation. To feel that time has become hastier, even as the interval remaining narrows, is a vertigo to which the Gnostic religion is almost uniquely fit to minister. Time, according to Judaism, Christianity, and Islam, is the mercy of Eternity: it is redemptive. That purports to be another beautiful idealism, and yet it is a lie, one that profoundly works against the spark that can help to hinder our hastening to a nihilistic consummation.

What the Gnosis tells us is that time, which degrades, itself is the product of a divine degradation, a failure within God. I have delayed speaking about the divine degradation until now, because no aspect of Gnosticism is more misunderstood, or more offends the pious of the established churches. But the crisis within the Pleroma, the disruption in the original Fullness, had to be mutual: when we crashed down into this world made by the inept angels, then God crashed also, coming down not with us, but in some stranger sphere, impossibly remote. There are (at least) two *kenomas,* two cosmological emptinesses: our world, *this* world, and the invisible spheres also formed in fright, as Herman Melville says in his very Gnostic masterpiece, *Moby-Dick.* In *those* waste places, God now wanders, himself an alien, a stranger, an exile, even as we wander here. Time, an envious shadow (as the Gnostic poet Shelley called it) fell from the Fullness onto our world. An equally envious shadow, a nameless one, hovers across the wandering God of the Abyss, not only cut off from us, as we are from him, but as helpless without us as we are without him.

What makes us free is the Gnosis
of what we are being freed

Since I address myself to the seekers, to those who are Gnostics whether they know it or not, I speak with a certain freedom. This warning is because, henceforward, I cannot speak without the risk of offending the devout who trust in the Covenant, if they are Jews; who believe that Jesus was the Christ, if they are Christians; or who affirm that Muhammad was the seal of prophets, if they have accepted Islam. The Gnosis of what we are being freed is the knowledge of the fallen God that Gnostics once called the Demiurge, or true Father of lies, the God of this world masquerading as Yahweh the Father. Those who love the God whose Creation simultaneously was our and this world's Fall have Saint Paul as their strongest precursor, particularly because he was profoundly tempted by Christian Gnosticism, but turned away from it. Protean as Paul was, he emphasized the distance between his Christian Faith and the Jewish Law so fiercely that Faith became the only blessing and the Law a curse, an antithesis that some ancient Gnostics interpreted as their own quarrel between Gnosis and Faith, a Faith from which they refused to disentangle the Torah, or Law. Against Gnosis, Paul sought to oppose what he called "love," a calling the quasi-Gnostic Friedrich Nietzsche revealed to be something rather different:

> The very word "Christianity" is a misunderstanding,— truth to tell, there never was more than one Christian, and he *died* on the Cross. The "gospel" *died* on the Cross. . . . It is

false to the point of nonsense to see in "faith," in the faith in salvation through Christ, the distinguishing trait of the Christian: the only thing that is Christian is the Christian mode of existence, a life *such* as he had who died on the Cross.

Of Paul himself, Nietzsche remarked: "The thought of union with Christ made him lose all shame, all submission, all constraint, and his ungovernable ambition was shown to be revelling in the expectation of divine glories." One can add George Bernard Shaw's observation as to Paul: "He is no more a Christian than Jesus was a Baptist; he is a disciple of Jesus only as Jesus was a disciple of John. He does nothing that Jesus would have done, and says nothing that Jesus would have said." If Christian "faith" means Paul, and almost inevitably it does, then Gnosis takes on its deepest meaning, which is a return to the origins, not of Christianity, but of the Pleroma, of the state in which God and the human are indistinguishable. Yet of what are we being freed: of the false remnant of God and the angels who were the residue after they broke unity with the human? In the Gnostic view, the God of the organized Western faiths is an impostor, no matter what name he assumes. His act of usurpation masked itself by renaming the original Fullness as the Abyss, or chaos, and by obscenely naming the Fall into division as the Creation. A divine degradation presents itself as a benign act; Gnosticism begins in the repudiation of this act, and in the knowledge that freedom depends upon a return to what preceded the Creation-Fall. Now we are forlorn, suffering from homesickness and dread, most frequently called "depression." Yet from a Gnostic perspective, our trauma is shock; having been thrown, we are stunned, and being victims of the lie, we forget what it is that we know. Knowledge ultimately is of the oldest part of your own deepest self, and that is knowledge of the best of your self. The Creation could not alter that best part; a spark in you even now is healed, original, pure. This spark is also a seed, and from it springs the unwavering Gnosis, which makes us free of what most men and women go on calling God, though the angel they worship as God is a poor ruin, dehumanized.

What makes us free is the Gnosis
of what birth really is

In *The Gospel of Thomas*, the Gnostic Jesus emphasizes that we never were created, and so there is no need for an end-time. We began before the beginning, and we will be here after the supposed Apocalypse. What then can your birth really have been, if what is oldest, best, and most yourself never passed through birth? Hear this exchange from *The Gospel of Thomas*, between an anonymous woman and Jesus:

> A woman in the crowd said to him, "Fortunate are the womb that bore you and the breasts that fed you."
> He said to her, "Fortunate are those who have heard the word of the father and have truly kept it. For there will be days when you will say, 'Fortunate are the womb that has not conceived and the breasts that have not given milk.'"

Elsewhere in *The Gospel of Thomas,* Jesus distinguishes between the "true" mother and the merely actual or natural
mother, and again in this collection of sayings he observes very
darkly: "Whoever knows the father and the mother will be
called the child of a whore," because it is an error to "know"
one's natural descent, which simply does not belong to Gnosis.
Only the spark or original self can be known, whether in oneself or in others. None of this questions or denounces fatherhood or motherhood as such; its effect rather is to free us by
seeing birth itself as a participation or renewal of the Creation-
Fall. This is not to lament or regret natural birth; it is a question
only of perspective. But that turns me to the heart of this sermon, for it is the center of Gnosis: what is the proper understanding of rebirth and of resurrection?

What makes us free is the Gnosis
of what rebirth really is

As intimated earlier, Gnosticism can be pagan, Jewish,
Christian, or Muslim, or can even take on the outer forms of
more Eastern spiritualities. Hermetists from ancient Alexandria
through the Italian Renaissance on to Giordano Bruno form
one continuous tradition of pagan Gnostics. Jewish Gnosticism
goes from the *minim* or heretics of Talmudic Palestine through
the vast Kabbalistic tradition, which remains vital today. Christian Gnosticism, extirpated by the Church, went underground
and emerged again as the Cathars of the late twelfth century onwards, only to be destroyed by a thirteenth-century papal crusade, in a campaign of extermination that is a crucial part of the

Catholic Church's long history of fraud and violence. The Gnosticism of the Muslim Sufis, particularly of the Shi'ites, has survived many persecutions in Islam, and will survive the barbarities of contemporary Iran. I mention all this because one cannot expound the Gnosis of rebirth without entering into the image of resurrection, and I wish to detach that image from Jesus, or rather from the Jesus of the dogmatic churches. What makes us free is finally the Gnosis of the Resurrection Body, whether the image known be that of Hermes, the angel Metatron in Kabbalah, the Angel Christ, or the various forms of the Man of Light in Iranian Sufism. All of these are versions of the Gnostic Anthropos; and what else is rebirth, and what else is resurrection?

In *The Gospel of Thomas*, as I interpret it, rebirth is associated with sharing the solitude of Jesus, or being a wayfarer with him. For the Gnostic Jesus has nothing to do with the Crucifixion; the "living Jesus" of *The Gospel of Thomas* has been resurrected without undergoing the sacrifice of Atonement. It is no fundamental fault of our own that we find ourselves solitaries in a cosmic jungle, our galaxy, cut off from salvation by the true God who has *not* made this world, has *not* made man's soul, has *not* even made the spark, or man's true self, because that is co-eternal with God. There is thus no basis for a sacrifice within God, or within man, and what James Joyce called the Hangman God of dogmatic Christianity is therefore irrelevant to the process of resurrection. When the ancient Gnostics were asked to confront the image of Christ upon the cross, they replied that it was an "apparition," and that the fiery spirit of Jesus could not suffer. Some said that the "laughing Savior" stood next to the cross, mocking the persecutors of his apparition or substitute.

Nothing seemed more sublimely crazy to Christian Gnostics than the Church's worship of an instrument of torture with which the degraded, false god had attempted to humiliate and destroy the Man of Light. Muslims were later to agree with this view, and I note that many indigenous American spiritual groups either discard the cross (as the Mormons do) or have only the bare cross with no one upon it, the Cross of the Resurrection. The Gnostic *Treatise on Resurrection* asks the meaning of the Resurrection, and replies: "It is the uncovering at any given time of the elements that have arisen." This "migration into newness" has taken place already within each Gnostic, and the Resurrection is therefore the Gnosis itself. The New Testament, in an act of amazing censorship, tells us almost nothing about the forty days and nights the Disciples traveled about in the company of Jesus *after his Resurrection*. If you consult the *Catholic Encyclopaedia* on this not unimportant matter, you will encounter only a polite discouragement as to further enquiry. But dogmatic Christianity abandoned those forty days from the start; Gnostics ancient and modern have reimagined them, and whether you are Christian Gnostic or purely a knower apart from all creed, I invite you to ponder them with me, and with all those from the ancient Valentinians to the modern Mormons who have declined to be discouraged by dogmatisms, polite or coercive. "While we exist in this world we must acquire resurrection," according to the Gnostic *Gospel of Philip*, and the poets have agreed: William Blake, Arthur Rimbaud, Rainer Maria Rilke, and so many others. Perhaps the Shi'ite Sufis have imagined most coherently and comprehensively in regard to the difficult image of the Resurrection Body; like the later Kabbalists after them, they had doctrines of alternative worlds, of varied states of being that intersect in this life. Perhaps Gnosis ultimately requires such complex theosophics, but this is a sermon on spiritual freedom, and so I want to attempt a much more direct vision of the image of rebirth or resurrection than Sufism or Kabbalah might permit me.

If the Gnosis makes us free, it can only be that it teaches us a resurrection that precedes death, even as *The Gospel of Philip* tells us of the Christ that "he first arose and then died." The principal, preparatory image that *The Gospel of Philip* (an anthology of Valentinian Gnosticism) employs for resurrection is "the bridal chamber," a Gnostic sacramental symbol for the lost, androgynous Fullness of the Pleroma. Bentley Layton remarks that we cannot be certain whether the Valentinian Gnostics actually celebrated a bridal chamber sacrament, or simply employed it as a spiritual image; either way, it retains a mythic force as a prelude to resurrection. I suspect that there was an enacted ritual of the bridal chamber, to restore the androgyne who was Anthropos, but whatever the sexual procedures may have been, the symbolic burden was the annihilation of death's realm. Except for *The Gospel of Truth*, we have only fragments of Valentinus, and this is one of them:

From the beginning you have been immortal, and you are children of eternal life. And you wanted death to be allocated to yourselves so that you might spend it and use it up, and that death might die in you and through you. For when you nullify the world and are not yourselves annihilated, you are lord over creation and all corruption.

This striking passage comes down to us with an illuminating commentary from Saint Clement of Alexandria, a great Christian intellectual who was a younger contemporary of Valentinus:

[Valentinus] supposed that there is a people that by its very nature is saved; that this race, indeed, has come down to us for the destruction of death; and that the origination of death is the work of the creator of the world.

I hardly see how the issue between Gnosticism and Christianity, between Valentinus and Clement, could be more clearly stated. Valentinus, greatest of Gnostics, tells us that there are the knowers of resurrection among us, and that they will annihilate death; Clement, defensively, expresses the shock of the Christian of faith, who finds that his God is held culpable for the invention of death. And *there* is the vital center of the endless conflict between Gnosticism and institutional Judaism, Christianity, and Islam: who is responsible for the origin of death, and what is the nature of the resurrection? If you can accept a God who coexists with death camps, schizophrenia, and AIDS, yet remains all-powerful and somehow benign, then you have faith, and you have accepted the Covenant with Yahweh, or the Atonement of Christ, or the submission to Islam. If you *know* yourself as having an affinity with the alien, or stranger God, cut off from this world, then you are a Gnostic, and perhaps the best and strongest moments still come to what is best and oldest in you, to a breath or spark that long precedes this Creation. In those moments, you do not know death; you know rather what Valentinus meant in the hushed awareness that concludes *The Gospel of Truth:*

> Such is the place of the blessed; this is their place. As for the others, then, may they know, in their place, that it does not suit me, after having been in the place of rest, to say anything more.

ACKNOWLEDGMENTS

I am greatly indebted to my editor, Celina Spiegel, and to my research assistants, Ginger Gaines and Carla Januska. As always, I am grateful to the libraries and librarians of Yale University.

—HAROLD BLOOM
February 6, 1996
Timothy Dwight College
Yale University